CHARLES VANCE

Ethical Hacking Volume 3

Powered by chatGPT

First edition

This book was professionally typeset on Reedsy.
Find out more at reedsy.com

Contents

Preface

As technology continues to advance, cybersecurity threats have become increasingly prevalent, sophisticated, and damaging. In this fast-paced and ever-changing landscape, it is essential to stay informed about the latest cybersecurity concepts, tools, and techniques.

This book, "Ethical Hacking - Volume 3: Scanning Concepts - Data/Device Protection," is the third volume in a series of comprehensive guides aimed at providing readers with a deeper understanding of cybersecurity and preparing them for the EC-Council CEF (Certified Encryption Specialist) exam.

In this volume, we focus on scanning concepts, which are fundamental to network security. We explore various scanning tools and techniques, including host discovery, port and service discovery, OS discovery, scanning beyond IDS and firewall, and drawing network diagrams. However, the book's unique feature is its emphasis on data and device protection.

We live in a world where data is the new currency. Hence, it is essential to learn how to secure our data and devices from cybercriminals who seek to exploit vulnerabilities for their gain. This volume provides a comprehensive understanding of how to protect data and devices using scanning techniques. The book provides practical examples and exercises to help readers understand how scanning concepts can be applied in an ethical hacking context.

We hope that this book will serve as an invaluable resource for cybersecurity professionals, network administrators, and anyone interested in improving their network security skills. Our goal is to provide a practical and accessible guide that will help readers achieve the EC-Council CEF certification and enhance their cybersecurity knowledge.

We would like to express our appreciation to our readers for choosing this book, and we hope that it will exceed your expectations. We invite you to join us on this exciting journey into the world of ethical hacking and network security.

1

Introduction to Network Scanning

Network scanning is the process of identifying active hosts, open ports, and services running on a network. It involves using specialized tools and techniques to probe a network and collect information about its devices, operating systems, and applications.

Network scanning is an essential component of network security. It helps organizations identify vulnerabilities and potential attack vectors, such as misconfigured systems, unpatched software, and open ports. By conducting regular network scans, organizations can detect potential security threats and take appropriate measures to prevent them.

Network scanning also plays a critical role in incident response and forensic investigations. When a security breach occurs, network scans can provide valuable information about the scope and impact of the attack. This information can help organizations identify the source of the breach, assess the damage, and develop a plan to mitigate the impact.

Overall, network scanning is a vital tool in the fight against cyber threats. It helps organizations stay one step ahead of potential attackers by identifying vulnerabilities before they can be exploited. By conducting regular network scans, organizations can maintain a strong security posture and protect their sensitive data and systems.

Types of Scanning

There are various types of network scanning techniques used by security professionals and IT administrators to assess and monitor network security. Some of the most common types of network scanning include:

1. Ping Scanning: Ping scanning is a basic technique that involves sending a ping request to each IP address on the network to identify active hosts.
2. Port Scanning: Port scanning is a technique that involves probing a network to determine which ports are open and which services are running on them.
3. Vulnerability Scanning: Vulnerability scanning involves scanning a network for known vulnerabilities and weaknesses in software, operating systems, and network devices.
4. Operating System Fingerprinting: Operating system fingerprinting is a technique used to determine the operating system running on a target device by analyzing the response to network packets sent to the device.
5. Service Scanning: Service scanning involves scanning a network for specific services or applications running on devices to identify potential security risks.
6. Web Application Scanning: Web application scanning involves scanning a network for vulnerabilities in web

applications and web servers.

7. Malware Scanning: Malware scanning involves scanning a network for malware infections and identifying potential security risks.

Each type of network scanning technique has its unique strengths and weaknesses. Combining different scanning techniques can provide a more comprehensive view of a network's security posture and help identify potential security risks.

Ping Scanning

Ping scanning is a type of network scanning technique that involves sending a ping request to each IP address on a network to identify active hosts. A ping request is a small packet of data sent from one device to another to check if it is online and available. If the target device is active and available, it will respond with a ping reply.

Ping scanning is a basic and fast method to identify active hosts on a network. It is often the first step in network reconnaissance to assess the scope of the network. Ping scanning is also useful in identifying rogue devices that are connected to the network without authorization. By identifying active hosts on a network, IT administrators and security professionals can ensure that all devices on the network are authorized and secure.

There are several ping scanning tools available, both commercial and open-source, that IT administrators and security professionals can use to identify active hosts on a network. Some of the most popular tools include Nmap, Fping, and Angry IP Scanner. These ping scanning tools can also provide additional information about the target devices, such as their hostname, MAC address, and response time. However, ping scanning has its limitations, as some devices may not respond to ping requests, and ping scanning cannot identify open ports or services running on devices. Therefore, other scanning techniques, such as port scanning or vulnerability scanning, may be necessary to conduct a comprehensive network assessment.

1. Nmap: Nmap is a free and open-source tool that can be used for ping scanning, port scanning, service detection, and vulnerability scanning. It is available for Windows, Mac OS, and Linux. Nmap can be downloaded from its official website at https://nmap.org/.

2. Fping: Fping is a free and open-source ping scanning tool that can scan multiple IP addresses simultaneously. It is available for Windows, Mac OS, and Linux. Fping can be downloaded from its official website at https://fping.org/.

3. Angry IP Scanner: Angry IP Scanner is a free and open-source tool that can scan IP addresses and ports to identify active hosts and services running on them. It is available for Windows, Mac OS, and Linux. Angry IP Scanner can be downloaded from its official website at https://angryip.or g/.

4. SolarWinds Ping Sweep Tool: SolarWinds Ping Sweep Tool is a free tool that can scan a range of IP addresses and identify active hosts on a network. It is available for Windows and can be downloaded from the SolarWinds website at https://www.solarwinds.com/free-tools/icmp-ping-sweep.

5. Advanced IP Scanner: Advanced IP Scanner is a free tool that can scan a network and identify active hosts and

devices. It is available for Windows and can be downloaded from its official website at https://www.advanced-ip-scanner.com/.

It's important to note that while these tools are useful for ping scanning, they should be used ethically and with permission. Unauthorized scanning of networks and devices can be considered illegal and can result in serious consequences. Therefore, it's essential to ensure that any network scanning activity is authorized and conducted within the limits of the law.

Port Scanning

Port scanning is a network scanning technique that involves probing a network to determine which ports are open and which services are running on them. A port is a communication endpoint used by devices to exchange data with other devices. Different types of services use specific ports to communicate, such as HTTP (port 80), SSH (port 22), and FTP (port 21).

Port scanning is a crucial technique for assessing network security because open ports and services can be potential entry points for attackers to exploit vulnerabilities and launch attacks. By identifying which ports are open, IT administrators and security professionals can take appropriate measures to secure their networks and prevent attacks.

There are various port scanning techniques available, including:

1. TCP Scan: This technique involves probing a network to determine which TCP ports are open and which services are running on them.

2. UDP Scan: This technique involves probing a network to determine which UDP ports are open and which services are running on them.
3. SYN Scan: This technique involves sending a SYN packet to a target device and analyzing its response to determine whether the port is open or closed.
4. FIN Scan: This technique involves sending a FIN packet to a target device and analyzing its response to determine whether the port is open or closed.
5. XMAS Scan: This technique involves sending a series of packets with various flags set to a target device and analyzing its response to determine whether the port is open or closed.

There are several port scanning tools available, including Nmap, Angry IP Scanner, and Masscan. However, it's essential to use port scanning techniques ethically and with permission. Unauthorized scanning of networks and devices can be considered illegal and can result in serious consequences.

Masscan is an open-source, high-speed port scanning tool designed for large-scale network scanning. It is developed and maintained by Robert Graham of Errata Security and is known for its speed and efficiency, capable of scanning millions of IP addresses per hour.

Masscan uses custom TCP/IP stack implementations to increase scanning speeds and bypasses rate-limiting mechanisms to deliver faster results. It can also detect firewall rules and filter policies that may be in place to block scanning activities.

In addition to port scanning, Masscan can also conduct service version detection and host fingerprinting, making it a useful tool for network reconnaissance and assessment.

Masscan is available for free and can be downloaded from its official website at https://github.com/robertdavidgraham/ masscan. The tool is compatible with Windows, Mac OS, and Linux operating systems. Since Masscan is a command-line tool, users need to have a basic understanding of command-line interfaces and syntax to use it effectively.

It's important to note that while Masscan is a powerful tool for network scanning, it should be used ethically and with permission. Unauthorized scanning of networks and devices can be considered illegal and can result in serious consequences. Therefore, it's essential to ensure that any network scanning activity is authorized and conducted within the limits of the law.

Vulnerability Scanning

Vulnerability scanning is a type of network scanning technique that is used to identify potential vulnerabilities and weaknesses in software, operating systems, and network devices. The goal of vulnerability scanning is to identify security weaknesses before they can be exploited by attackers to gain unauthorized access to a network or system.

Vulnerability scanning involves using specialized tools to scan a network for known vulnerabilities and weaknesses. These tools typically use a database of known vulnerabilities and scan the network to identify systems and devices that are vulnerable to known exploits. Some vulnerability scanning tools can also detect unknown vulnerabilities by analyzing network traffic and behavior.

Vulnerability scanning is a critical component of network security, as it helps organizations identify and mitigate potential security risks. By conducting regular vulnerability scans, IT administrators and security professionals can ensure that their systems are up-to-date with the latest security patches and updates. They can also prioritize and remediate vulnerabilities that pose the most significant risk to their network.

There are several vulnerability scanning tools available, including Nessus, OpenVAS, and Qualys. Some of these tools are free and open-source, while others are commercial and require a license. It's important to use vulnerability scanning tools ethically and with permission. Unauthorized scanning of networks and devices can be considered illegal and can result in serious consequences. Therefore, it's essential to ensure that any vulnerability scanning activity is authorized and conducted within the limits of the law.

Here are some of the most popular vulnerability scanning tools used by IT administrators and security professionals:

1. Nessus: Nessus is a popular commercial vulnerability scanning tool developed by Tenable. It can scan a network for known vulnerabilities and provide detailed reports on the results. Nessus is available for Windows, Mac OS, and Linux operating systems. A free version of Nessus, called Nessus Essentials, is available for small networks. The commercial version can be purchased on the Tenable website at https://www.tenable.com/products/nessus.

2. OpenVAS: OpenVAS (Open Vulnerability Assessment System) is a free and open-source vulnerability scanning tool that can scan a network for known vulnerabilities and provide reports on the results. OpenVAS is available for Windows, Mac OS, and Linux operating systems. It can be downloaded from its official website at http://www.openvas.org/.

3. Qualys: Qualys is a cloud-based vulnerability scanning tool that can scan a network for known vulnerabilities and provide detailed reports on the results. Qualys offers both free and commercial versions of its product. The commercial version can be purchased on the Qualys website at https://www.qualys.com/.

4. Nexpose: Nexpose is a vulnerability scanning tool developed by Rapid7 that can scan a network for known vulnerabilities and provide detailed reports on the results. Nexpose is available for Windows, Mac OS, and Linux operating systems. The commercial version can be purchased on the Rapid7 website at https://www.rapid7.com/produc ts/nexpose/.

5. Retina: Retina is a vulnerability scanning tool developed by BeyondTrust that can scan a network for known vulnerabilities and provide detailed reports on the results. Retina is available for Windows operating systems. The commercial version can be purchased on the BeyondTrust website at https://www.beyondtrust.com/products/retin a-vulnerability-management.

It's important to note that while these vulnerability scanning tools are useful for identifying potential security risks, they should be used ethically and with permission. Unauthorized scanning of networks and devices can be considered illegal and can result in serious consequences. Therefore, it's essential to ensure that any vulnerability scanning activity is authorized and conducted within the limits of the law.

Operating System Fingerprinting

Operating system fingerprinting is a network scanning technique used to determine the operating system running on a target device by analyzing the response to network packets sent to the device. This technique is based on the fact that different operating systems respond differently to the same network packets.

Operating system fingerprinting involves sending a series of network packets to the target device and analyzing its response to determine the operating system running on the device. The packets sent may include TCP packets with various flags set, ICMP packets, or UDP packets. The response to these packets can provide information about the operating system, including its version number, patch level, and installed services.

Operating system fingerprinting can provide valuable information to IT administrators and security professionals, such as identifying unpatched or outdated operating systems that may be vulnerable to attacks. It can also help identify rogue or unauthorized devices on a network.

There are several tools available for operating system fingerprinting, including Nmap, Xprobe2, and p0f. These tools can be used to identify the operating system of a target device by analyzing its response to network packets. However, it's important to use operating system fingerprinting tools ethically and with permission. Unauthorized scanning of networks and devices can be considered illegal and can result in serious consequences. Therefore, it's essential to ensure that any network scanning activity is authorized and conducted within the limits of the law.

Here are some of the most popular tools used for operating system fingerprinting:

1. Nmap: Nmap is a free and open-source tool that can be used for network scanning, including operating system fingerprinting. It is available for Windows, Mac OS, and Linux. Nmap can be downloaded from its official website at https://nmap.org/.
2. Xprobe2: Xprobe2 is a free and open-source tool used for remote operating system detection. It can be used to identify the operating system running on a target device by analyzing its response to various network probes. Xprobe2 is available for Windows, Mac OS, and Linux. It can be downloaded from its official website at http://www.sys-security.com/html/projects/X.html.
3. p0f: p0f is a passive operating system fingerprinting tool that analyzes network traffic to identify the operating system running on a target device. It is free and open-source and available for Windows, Mac OS, and Linux. It can be downloaded from its official website at https://lca mtuf.coredump.cx/p0f3/.
4. Ettercap: Ettercap is a free and open-source network security tool that can be used for various tasks, including operating system fingerprinting. It can analyze network traffic to identify the operating system running on a target device. Ettercap is available for Windows, Mac OS, and Linux. It can be downloaded from its official website at https://ettercap.github.io/ettercap/.

It's important to note that while these tools are useful for operating system fingerprinting, they should be used ethically and with permission. Unauthorized scanning of networks and devices can be considered illegal and can result in serious consequences. Therefore, it's essential to ensure that any network scanning activity is authorized and conducted within the limits of the law.

Service Scanning

Service scanning is a type of network scanning technique used to identify services running on a target device or network. It involves probing a network to determine which services are running on which ports and what version of the service is running.

Service scanning is a crucial technique for assessing network security because it helps IT administrators and security professionals identify potential vulnerabilities in services running on devices. Attackers can exploit vulnerabilities in services to gain unauthorized access to a network or system.

There are several tools available for service scanning, including Nmap, OpenVAS, and Nessus. These tools can be used to identify services running on a target device or network by analyzing their response to network probes.

Service scanning can also help identify unauthorized or rogue services running on a network. This information can be used to detect and remove any potentially malicious services that may have been installed by attackers.

It's important to use service scanning tools ethically and with permission. Unauthorized scanning of networks and devices can be considered illegal and can result in serious consequences. Therefore, it's essential to ensure that any network scanning activity is authorized and conducted within the limits of the law.

Here are some of the most popular tools used for service scanning:

1. Nmap: Nmap is a free and open-source tool that can be used for network scanning, including service scanning. It is available for Windows, Mac OS, and Linux. Nmap can be downloaded from its official website at https://nmap.org/.
2. OpenVAS: OpenVAS (Open Vulnerability Assessment System) is a free and open-source vulnerability scanning tool that can also be used for service scanning. It can scan a network for known vulnerabilities and services running on devices. OpenVAS is available for Windows, Mac OS, and Linux operating systems. It can be downloaded from its official website at http://www.openvas.org/.
3. Nessus: Nessus is a popular commercial vulnerability scanning tool that can also be used for service scanning. It can scan a network for known vulnerabilities and services running on devices. Nessus is available for Windows, Mac OS, and Linux operating systems. A free version of Nessus, called Nessus Essentials, is available for small networks. The commercial version can be purchased on the Tenable website at https://www.tenable.com/products/nessus.
4. Netcat: Netcat is a free and open-source tool that can be used for service scanning. It can be used to scan for open ports and services running on a target device. Netcat is available for Windows, Mac OS, and Linux operating systems. It can be downloaded from its official website at https://eternallybored.org/misc/netcat/.

It's important to note that while these tools are useful for service scanning, they should be used ethically and with permission.

Unauthorized scanning of networks and devices can be considered illegal and can result in serious consequences. Therefore, it's essential to ensure that any network scanning activity is authorized and conducted within the limits of the law.

Web application scanning

Web application scanning is a type of network scanning technique used to identify potential vulnerabilities in web applications running on a network. It involves sending specially crafted HTTP requests to web applications to identify vulnerabilities that can be exploited by attackers.

Web application scanning can identify vulnerabilities such as SQL injection, cross-site scripting (XSS), directory traversal, and file inclusion vulnerabilities. These vulnerabilities can be exploited by attackers to steal sensitive data, compromise web servers, and gain unauthorized access to network resources.

There are several tools available for web application scanning, including Burp Suite, Acunetix, and OWASP ZAP. These tools can be used to identify vulnerabilities in web applications by analyzing the responses to HTTP requests.

Web application scanning is essential for securing web applications and preventing attacks on web servers. By identifying and remediating vulnerabilities, IT administrators and security professionals can reduce the risk of data breaches and other cyber attacks.

It's important to use web application scanning tools ethically and with permission. Unauthorized scanning of web applications can be considered illegal and can result in serious consequences. Therefore, it's essential to ensure that any web application scanning activity is authorized and conducted within the limits of the law.

Here are some of the most popular tools used for web application scanning:

1. Burp Suite: Burp Suite is a popular web application security testing tool that can be used for web application scanning. It is developed by PortSwigger and is available in both a free and a paid version. Burp Suite can be used to identify vulnerabilities such as SQL injection, cross-site scripting (XSS), and file inclusion vulnerabilities. Burp Suite is available for Windows, Mac OS, and Linux operating systems. It can be downloaded from its official website at https://portswigger.net/burp.

2. Acunetix: Acunetix is a commercial web vulnerability scanner that can be used for web application scanning. It can identify vulnerabilities such as SQL injection, cross-site scripting (XSS), and file inclusion vulnerabilities. Acunetix is available for Windows and Linux operating systems. The commercial version can be purchased on the Acunetix website at https://www.acunetix.com/.

3. OWASP ZAP: OWASP ZAP (Zed Attack Proxy) is a free and open-source web application scanner that can be used for web application scanning. It can identify vulnerabilities such as SQL injection, cross-site scripting (XSS), and file inclusion vulnerabilities. OWASP ZAP is available for Windows, Mac OS, and Linux operating systems. It can be downloaded from its official website at https://www.zaproxy.org/.

4. Nikto: Nikto is a free and open-source web server scanner that can be used for web application scanning. It can iden-

tify vulnerabilities such as outdated server software, server misconfigurations, and vulnerable web applications. Nikto is available for Windows, Mac OS, and Linux operating systems. It can be downloaded from its official website at https://cirt.net/Nikto2.

It's important to note that while these tools are useful for web application scanning, they should be used ethically and with permission. Unauthorized scanning of web applications can be considered illegal and can result in serious consequences. Therefore, it's essential to ensure that any web application scanning activity is authorized and conducted within the limits of the law.

Malware Scanning

Malware scanning is a type of network scanning technique used to identify malware and other malicious code that may be present on a network or device. Malware scanning involves scanning files, directories, and network traffic for signs of malware infections or suspicious behavior.

Malware scanning can help IT administrators and security professionals detect and remove malware infections before they cause damage to network resources or sensitive data. It can also help identify and remove unauthorized or malicious software that may have been installed on devices by attackers.

There are several tools available for malware scanning, including antivirus software, anti-malware software, and specialized malware scanners. These tools can scan files, directories, and network traffic for signs of malware infections or suspicious behavior.

Some popular malware scanning tools include:

1. Malwarebytes: Malwarebytes is a popular anti-malware tool that can be used for malware scanning. It can scan files, directories, and network traffic for signs of malware infections. Malwarebytes is available for Windows, Mac OS, and Linux operating systems. The commercial version can be purchased on the Malwarebytes website at https://www.malwarebytes.com/.

2. Microsoft Defender: Microsoft Defender is a free antivirus software developed by Microsoft that can be used for malware scanning. It can scan files and directories for malware infections and suspicious behavior. Microsoft Defender is built into Windows 10 and can be enabled in the Windows Security settings.

3. ClamAV: ClamAV is a free and open-source antivirus software that can be used for malware scanning. It can scan files, directories, and network traffic for signs of malware infections. ClamAV is available for Windows, Mac OS, and Linux operating systems. It can be downloaded from its official website at https://www.clamav.net/.

4. ESET Online Scanner: ESET Online Scanner is a free online malware scanner that can scan a device for malware infections. It can scan files, directories, and network traffic for signs of malware infections. ESET Online Scanner can be accessed through its official website at https://www.eset.com/us/home/online-scanner/.

It's important to use malware scanning tools ethically and with permission. Unauthorized scanning of devices can be considered illegal and can result in serious consequences. Therefore, it's essential to ensure that any malware scanning activity is authorized and conducted within the limits of the law.

Scanning Process Overview

The network scanning process involves systematically examining a network to identify active devices, open ports, and potential vulnerabilities. The process typically involves the following steps:

1. Planning: Define the objectives of the network scan, identify the scope of the scan, and obtain the necessary permissions to conduct the scan.
2. Host discovery: Identify active devices on the network using tools such as ping scans or ARP scans.
3. Port scanning: Identify open ports on the active devices using tools such as Nmap, Masscan, or Netcat.
4. Service scanning: Identify services running on open ports using tools such as Nmap, OpenVAS, or Nessus.
5. Vulnerability scanning: Identify vulnerabilities in services or applications using tools such as Burp Suite, Acunetix, or OWASP ZAP.
6. Operating system fingerprinting: Identify the operating system running on target devices using tools such as Nmap, Xprobe2, or p0f.
7. Malware scanning: Scan files, directories, and network traffic for signs of malware infections or suspicious behavior using tools such as antivirus software or anti-malware software.
8. Analysis: Analyze the results of the network scan and prioritize any identified vulnerabilities based on their

severity.

9. Reporting: Document the results of the network scan and provide recommendations for remediation.

It's important to use network scanning tools ethically and with permission. Unauthorized scanning of networks and devices can be considered illegal and can result in serious consequences. Therefore, it's essential to ensure that any network scanning activity is authorized and conducted within the limits of the law.

Planning

Planning is a critical step in the network scanning process. It involves defining the objectives of the network scan, identifying the scope of the scan, and obtaining the necessary permissions to conduct the scan. Here are some of the key considerations in the planning phase of network scanning:

1. Define the objectives: Clearly define the objectives of the network scan, such as identifying potential vulnerabilities, detecting malware infections, or evaluating network performance. This will help determine which scanning techniques and tools are most appropriate for achieving the desired results.
2. Identify the scope: Determine the scope of the network scan, including the network range or IP addresses to be scanned, the devices or systems to be scanned, and the time frame for conducting the scan.
3. Obtain permissions: Obtain the necessary permissions to conduct the network scan. This may involve getting approval from senior management, the IT department,

or other stakeholders. It's important to ensure that any network scanning activity is authorized and conducted within the limits of the law.

4. Consider the impact: Consider the potential impact of the network scan on the network and the devices being scanned. Scanning can cause network congestion or impact system performance. It's important to schedule the scan during off-peak hours and to notify affected users or stakeholders in advance.

5. Prepare the scanning tools: Ensure that the necessary scanning tools are available and properly configured. This may involve installing and configuring software, updating virus definitions, or configuring network settings.

By carefully planning the network scan, IT administrators and security professionals can ensure that the scanning process is conducted efficiently and effectively while minimizing any potential impact on the network and its users.

Host discovery

Host discovery is the process of identifying active devices on a network. It is typically the first step in the network scanning process and involves sending probes to target devices to determine whether they are active and can respond to network requests.

Here are some of the common techniques used for host discovery:

1. Ping Scanning: Ping scanning involves sending an ICMP

echo request to a device to determine whether it is active and responsive. Tools such as Nmap, Fping, and Angry IP Scanner can be used for ping scanning.

2. ARP Scanning: ARP scanning involves sending ARP requests to devices on a local network to determine their IP addresses and MAC addresses. Tools such as ARP Scan, Netdiscover, and Angry IP Scanner can be used for ARP scanning.

3. Reverse DNS Lookup: Reverse DNS lookup involves querying a DNS server to resolve an IP address to a hostname. This technique can be used to identify the hostnames of active devices on a network.

4. Passive Discovery: Passive discovery involves monitoring network traffic to identify active devices. This technique can be useful for detecting devices that may not respond to active scanning techniques.

Host discovery is an important step in the network scanning process as it helps identify the devices that will be included in the subsequent scanning steps. By identifying active devices on a network, IT administrators and security professionals can ensure that they are scanning all devices on the network and can detect potential vulnerabilities or security issues.

Scanning has already been discussed in detail.

Analysis and Reporting

Analysis and reporting are the final steps in the network scanning process. After completing the network scan, IT administrators and security professionals must analyze the results of the scan and generate a report detailing the findings and recommendations for remediation.

Here are some of the key considerations in the analysis and reporting phase of network scanning:

1. Prioritize vulnerabilities: Review the results of the scan and prioritize any identified vulnerabilities based on their severity. This will help focus remediation efforts on the most critical issues.
2. Determine remediation steps: Identify the steps needed to remediate any identified vulnerabilities. This may involve patching systems, updating software, or changing configuration settings.
3. Generate a report: Document the results of the network scan in a report that details the findings, vulnerabilities, and recommended remediation steps. The report should be clear, concise, and provide actionable information for remediation.
4. Present the report: Present the report to relevant stake-holders, such as senior management, the IT department, or other relevant parties. This will help ensure that any identified vulnerabilities are properly addressed and that the network is secure.

By analyzing the results of the network scan and generating a report, IT administrators and security professionals can identify potential vulnerabilities and take steps to remediate them before they can be exploited by attackers. The analysis and reporting phase is critical in ensuring the overall security and integrity of the network.

Discussion

Ethical considerations are crucial when conducting network scanning activities. One key ethical consideration is obtaining permission from the appropriate authorities to conduct the scan. Conducting unauthorized scans can be considered illegal and can have serious legal consequences. Additionally, network scanning activities should be conducted within the limits of the law, including compliance with data privacy and confidentiality laws. Another ethical consideration is avoiding causing unnecessary harm or disruption to the network. Scans should be carefully planned and conducted in a way that minimizes the impact on the network and its users.

Ping scanning is a common network scanning technique that involves sending an ICMP echo request to a device to determine whether it is active and responsive. However, ping scanning has limitations in that it cannot identify open ports or services running on devices, and some devices may not respond to ping requests. Therefore, other scanning techniques such as port scanning or vulnerability scanning may be necessary to conduct a comprehensive network assessment.

Port scanning is an important part of the network scanning process as it helps identify the open ports on devices that can potentially be exploited by attackers. By identifying open ports and the services running on them, IT administrators and security professionals can take steps to secure their networks and prevent potential attacks. Common techniques used for service scanning include banner grabbing, protocol scanning, and operating system fingerprinting.

Potential risks associated with network scanning activities include the possibility of network congestion or impact on system performance, the potential for triggering intrusion detection systems (IDS) or firewalls, and the potential for legal consequences if conducted without permission. It's important to conduct network scanning activities ethically and with permission to avoid these risks.

Malware scanning is important as it can help detect and remove malware infections before they cause damage to network resources or sensitive data. Popular tools used for vulnerability scanning include Burp Suite, Acunetix, and OWASP ZAP. Operating system fingerprinting is important in the network scanning process as it helps identify the specific operating system running on target devices, which can provide valuable information about potential vulnerabilities and security issues associated with specific operating systems.

Key considerations in the analysis and reporting phase of network scanning include prioritizing vulnerabilities, determining remediation steps, generating a clear and concise report, and presenting the report to relevant stakeholders. Benefits of network scanning for IT administrators and security professionals include identifying potential vulnerabilities, detecting malware infections, evaluating network performance, and taking steps to secure networks and prevent potential attacks.

Quiz (Solutions in Appendix)

1. What are some of the ethical considerations when conducting network scanning activities?
2. What are some of the limitations of ping scanning?
3. Why is port scanning an important part of the network scanning process?
4. What are some of the common techniques used for service

scanning?

5. What are some of the potential risks associated with net-work scanning activities?

6. What is malware scanning and why is it important?

7. What are some of the popular tools used for vulnerability scanning?

8. Why is operating system fingerprinting important in the network scanning process?

9. What are some of the key considerations in the analysis and reporting phase of network scanning?

10. What are some of the benefits of network scanning for IT administrators and security professionals?

2

Scanning Tools

There are many scanning tools available to IT administrators and security professionals for network scanning. Here are some commonly used scanning tools:

1. Nmap: Nmap is a popular open-source scanning tool used for host discovery, port scanning, and service identification. It can be used for both TCP and UDP scanning and can provide detailed information about target devices.
2. Masscan: Masscan is a high-speed port scanning tool that can scan the entire internet in under six minutes. It is ideal for scanning large networks and can be used to identify open ports and services running on devices.
3. Nessus: Nessus is a widely used vulnerability scanning tool that can identify security vulnerabilities and configuration issues on target devices. It can be used to conduct both remote and authenticated scans.
4. OpenVAS: OpenVAS is an open-source vulnerability scanner that can identify potential security issues on target devices. It includes a web-based interface for managing

scans and generating reports.

5. Metasploit: Metasploit is a penetration testing framework that includes a wide range of scanning and exploitation tools. It can be used for both manual and automated testing and includes features for generating reports and tracking remediation efforts.

6. Burp Suite: Burp Suite is a web application testing tool that includes a scanner for identifying vulnerabilities in web applications. It can identify issues such as SQL injection, cross-site scripting (XSS), and other common web application vulnerabilities.

7. Nikto: Nikto is an open-source web server scanner that can identify potential vulnerabilities and misconfigurations on web servers. It can be used to identify issues such as outdated software versions, weak passwords, and default configurations.

These are just a few examples of commonly used scanning tools. There are many other tools available, both commercial and open-source, that can be used for network scanning and security testing.

Common Uses

1. Nmap: An IT administrator may use Nmap to perform a network scan of their organization's network to identify any active devices and open ports. They may use Nmap's service detection feature to identify the services running on each open port to ensure they are up-to-date and secure.

2. Masscan: A security professional may use Masscan to scan a large network for open ports and services running on

target devices. Masscan is a high-speed port scanner that can quickly identify open ports on a large network.

3. Nessus: A security professional may use Nessus to perform a vulnerability scan of a target device or network. Nessus can identify potential security vulnerabilities and configuration issues that could be exploited by attackers.

4. OpenVAS: An IT administrator may use OpenVAS to perform a vulnerability scan of their organization's network to identify potential security issues. OpenVAS is an open-source vulnerability scanner that can be used to identify common vulnerabilities and configuration issues.

5. Metasploit: A penetration tester may use Metasploit to identify vulnerabilities in a target system or network and attempt to exploit them. Metasploit includes a wide range of scanning and exploitation tools that can be used to test the security of a system.

6. Burp Suite: A web application developer may use Burp Suite to scan their web application for potential security vulnerabilities. Burp Suite includes a scanner that can identify common web application vulnerabilities such as SQL injection, cross-site scripting (XSS), and others.

7. Nikto: A security professional may use Nikto to perform a web server scan of a target website or web server. Nikto can identify potential security vulnerabilities and misconfigurations that could be exploited by attackers.

Features and capabilities

Scanning tools have a range of features and capabilities that make them useful for identifying potential security vulnerabilities and misconfigurations on target devices and networks.

Some common features and capabilities of scanning tools include:

1. Host discovery: Many scanning tools include features for identifying active hosts on a network. This can help IT administrators and security professionals identify potential entry points for attackers.
2. Port scanning: Scanning tools can identify open ports on devices, which can help identify potential vulnerabilities and misconfigurations that could be exploited by attackers.
3. Service scanning: Scanning tools can identify the services running on open ports on target devices. This can help identify potential vulnerabilities and ensure that services are up-to-date and secure.
4. Vulnerability scanning: Many scanning tools include features for identifying potential security vulnerabilities and configuration issues on target devices. This can help IT administrators and security professionals prioritize remediation efforts and improve overall security.
5. Malware scanning: Scanning tools can identify malware and other malicious code that may be present on a network or device. This can help detect and remove malware infections before they cause damage to network resources or sensitive data.
6. Web application scanning: Scanning tools can identify potential security vulnerabilities in web applications, such as SQL injection, cross-site scripting (XSS), and others. This can help web application developers ensure that their applications are secure.
7. Operating system fingerprinting: Scanning tools can identify the specific operating system running on target de-

vices, which can provide valuable information about potential vulnerabilities and security issues associated with
specific operating systems.

These are just a few examples of the features and capabilities
of scanning tools. Different tools have different strengths and
weaknesses, and it is important to choose the right tool for the
specific scanning task at hand.

Tool Selection

Selecting the right scanning tool for your needs requires careful
consideration of a range of factors. Here are some key considerations to keep in mind when selecting a scanning tool:

1. Scanning objectives: Consider your scanning objectives
   and the specific tasks you need the tool to perform. For
   example, do you need to perform a network scan to identify
   active hosts and open ports, or do you need to perform a
   web application scan to identify potential vulnerabilities
   in a web application?
2. Platform support: Consider the platforms that the scanning tool supports. Does it support the operating system
   and applications that you need to scan?
3. Ease of use: Consider the ease of use of the tool. Is it easy
   to set up and configure, or does it require a high level of
   technical expertise?
4. Cost: Consider the cost of the tool. Is it within your budget,
   or are there open-source alternatives that can provide
   similar functionality?
5. Integration: Consider how well the tool integrates with

other tools and systems in your organization. Can it be easily integrated with your existing security infrastructure?

6. Support: Consider the level of support provided by the tool's vendor. Is there a support team available to help you if you encounter issues, or are you on your own?

By carefully considering these factors, you can select a scanning tool that is well-suited to your needs and can help you achieve your scanning objectives. It is important to choose a tool that is reliable, easy to use, and provides the features and functionality that you need to identify potential security vulnerabilities and misconfigurations on your target devices and networks.

Attack Scenarios and Counter Measures

Scenario 1: A company's web application is vulnerable to SQL injection attacks, which could allow an attacker to extract sensitive information from the company's database.

Attack Vector: SQL injection attacks exploit vulnerabilities in web applications that do not properly sanitize user input, allowing an attacker to inject malicious SQL code into the application's backend database. This can allow the attacker to access sensitive information, modify or delete data, or even take control of the application.

Countermeasure: Ethical hackers can use web application scanning tools like Burp Suite or Nikto to identify potential vulnerabilities in the company's web application. Once the vulnerability is identified, the ethical hacker can work with the company's developers to implement secure coding practices and mitigate the vulnerability, such as using parameterized queries or input validation to prevent SQL injection attacks.

31

Other countermeasures can include implementing strict user authentication and authorization mechanisms and conducting regular security testing to identify and remediate potential vulnerabilities.

Scenario 2: An attacker gains access to a company's network through a phishing email or a weak password, and then attempts to escalate their privileges and gain access to sensitive information or systems.

Attack Vector: Phishing emails are a common attack vector used to trick users into divulging sensitive information or granting access to their accounts. Weak passwords or easily guessable credentials can also be exploited by attackers to gain access to systems and sensitive data.

Countermeasure: Ethical hackers can use vulnerability scanning tools like Nessus or OpenVAS to identify potential vulnerabilities on the company's network and take steps to patch those vulnerabilities to prevent unauthorized access. Additionally, ethical hackers can use penetration testing tools like Metasploit to simulate attacks and identify potential entry points that could be exploited by attackers. Countermeasures can include implementing strong password policies, conducting regular security training and awareness for employees to avoid phishing attacks, implementing multi-factor authentication, and continuously monitoring network traffic for suspicious activity.

Scenario 3: An attacker uses a port scanning tool like Nmap or Masscan to identify open ports and services running on the company's network, then attempts to exploit vulnerabilities in those services.

Attack Vector: Port scanning tools are used by attackers to identify open ports and services running on a network, which can be used to identify potential vulnerabilities that can be exploited to gain unauthorized access or steal sensitive information. Exploitation of these vulnerabilities can range from stealing login credentials, planting malware, or taking control of systems.

Countermeasure: Ethical hackers can use network scanning tools to identify potential vulnerabilities and then take steps to secure those services, such as applying software patches or disabling unnecessary services. Ethical hackers can also use intrusion detection and prevention systems (IDPS) to detect and block potential attacks on the company's network. Additionally, ethical hackers can use network monitoring tools to monitor network traffic and detect potential attacks before they cause damage. Other countermeasures include implementing network segmentation, implementing firewalls, and conducting regular security testing to identify and remediate potential vulnerabilities.

Tool selection is an essential aspect of network security testing, and it is essential to choose the right tools for the specific scenarios being tested. In the scenarios mentioned above, the ethical hacker would need to select tools that are appropriate for the particular attack vectors they are trying to counter.

For the SQL injection scenario, the ethical hacker could use web application scanning tools like Burp Suite or Nikto, which can identify potential vulnerabilities in web applications and recommend remediation steps. These tools can help the ethical hacker to identify vulnerabilities that could be exploited through SQL injection attacks, and suggest coding practices that could be implemented to mitigate the vulnerability.

For the phishing and weak password scenario, the ethical hacker could use vulnerability scanning tools like Nessus or OpenVAS to identify potential vulnerabilities on the company's network. These tools can help the ethical hacker to identify potential entry points that could be exploited by attackers, such as open ports or outdated software, and suggest remediation steps to mitigate these vulnerabilities. The ethical hacker could also use penetration testing tools like Metasploit to simulate attacks and identify potential vulnerabilities in the network.

For the port scanning scenario, the ethical hacker could use network scanning tools like Nmap or Masscan to identify potential vulnerabilities in the company's network. These tools can help the ethical hacker to identify open ports and services running on the network, which could be exploited by attackers to gain unauthorized access or steal sensitive information. The ethical hacker could then use intrusion detection and prevention systems (IDPS) to detect and block potential attacks on the company's network.

Overall, tool selection is a crucial aspect of network security testing, and it is essential to choose the right tools for the specific scenarios being tested. Ethical hackers should be trained to choose tools that are appropriate for the specific attack vectors they are trying to counter and to use these tools in a controlled and ethical manner. They should also follow legal and ethical guidelines and obtain permission from the company or organization being tested before conducting any security testing.

Discussion

Network scanning is an essential component of network security testing and helps to identify potential vulnerabilities,
detect malware infections, and evaluate network performance.
Scanning tools like Burp Suite, Nessus, OpenVAS, and Nmap
are popular for vulnerability assessment. Each tool has unique
features and capabilities that differentiate it from others. Burp
Suite is a web application scanning tool, Nessus and OpenVAS
are vulnerability scanners, and Nmap is a network scanning
tool.

Scanning tools can identify potential security risks and vulnerabilities in a network. For instance, ethical hackers can use
Nmap or Burp Suite to identify open ports and services running
on a network, and then use Nessus or OpenVAS to identify
potential vulnerabilities. By using these tools, ethical hackers
can help organizations identify and address vulnerabilities that
could be exploited by attackers.

Conducting network scanning activities requires ethical considerations to avoid unnecessary harm or disruption to the
network. Ethical hackers need to obtain permission to conduct
the scan and conduct the scan within the limits of the law. They
must take measures to mitigate the potential risks associated
with scanning, such as conducting scans during off-peak hours
and using scanning tools that allow for customization of scan
parameters.

Operating system fingerprinting is another important aspect
of network scanning. It helps identify the specific operating
system running on target devices, which can provide valuable
information about potential vulnerabilities and security issues
associated with specific operating systems. Ethical hackers can

use operating system fingerprinting tools like Nmap or Pof to identify the operating system running on a device.

Scanning tools can be used to identify malware infections on a network. Malware scanning tools like Malwarebytes or McAfee can help identify malware infections on a network, and then take steps to remove the malware and prevent further infections. By detecting and removing malware infections, organizations can prevent significant harm to their network resources and sensitive data.

When selecting scanning tools for network security testing, various considerations should be taken into account. For instance, the specific vulnerabilities and attack vectors being targeted, the level of customization and control needed, and the cost and availability of the tool. By selecting the appropriate scanning tool for the job, organizations can identify potential vulnerabilities and secure their network resources effectively.

Quiz (Solutions in Appendix)

1. What are the most popular scanning tools used for vulnerability assessment, and how do they differ from each other?
2. How can ethical hackers use scanning tools to identify potential security risks and vulnerabilities in a network?
3. What are some of the ethical considerations that should be taken into account when conducting network scanning activities?
4. How can operating system fingerprinting be used to identify potential vulnerabilities in a network?
5. What are some of the potential risks associated with conducting network scanning activities, and how can they be

mitigated?

6. How can scanning tools be used to identify malware infections on a network?

7. What are some of the benefits of network scanning for IT
   administrators and security professionals?

8. How can network scanning tools be used to identify potential entry points for attackers to exploit?

9. What are some of the considerations that should be taken
   into account when selecting scanning tools for network
   security testing?

10. How can ethical hackers use network scanning tools to col-
    laborate with development teams to improve the security
    of web applications?

3

Host Discovery

Host discovery is the first step in the network scanning process, and it involves identifying active hosts on a network. The host discovery process can be conducted using several techniques, including ping scanning, ARP scanning, and DNS querying. Ping scanning is the most common technique and involves sending an ICMP echo request to the target device and waiting for a response. ARP scanning is used on local networks to identify devices by sending ARP requests and mapping the MAC addresses to IP addresses. DNS querying involves querying the DNS server to obtain information about the target device.

The host discovery process is important as it helps IT administrators and security professionals identify active hosts on a network and determine the scope of the network assessment. Without host discovery, network scanning may miss important hosts or scan unnecessary devices, which can lead to inaccurate results and a waste of resources.

However, host discovery has its limitations, as some devices may not respond to ping requests or may have ICMP packets blocked by firewalls. In these cases, other techniques, such as

ARP scanning or DNS querying, may be necessary to identify the target device. Additionally, host discovery may generate network traffic, which can cause congestion or impact system performance. Therefore, it is important to conduct the host discovery process during off-peak hours or use scanning tools that allow for customization of scan parameters to avoid unnecessary network traffic.

Generally, the host discovery process is a crucial step in the network scanning process as it helps IT administrators and security professionals identify active hosts on a network and determine the scope of the network assessment. By using a combination of host discovery techniques, including ping scanning, ARP scanning, and DNS querying, IT professionals can accurately identify active hosts on a network and ensure that their scanning activities are targeted and effective.

Techniques

There are several techniques that can be used for host discovery, including ping scanning, ARP scanning, and DNS zone transfers. Ping scanning involves sending an ICMP (Internet Control Message Protocol) echo request to a target device and waiting for a response to determine if the device is active. ARP scanning involves sending an ARP (Address Resolution Protocol) request to a target device and waiting for a response to determine if the device is active. DNS zone transfers involve querying a DNS (Domain Name System) server for a list of all the hosts within a specific domain.

Another technique for host discovery is using port scanning tools like Nmap or Angry IP Scanner. These tools can scan a range of IP addresses and identify which hosts are active based

39

on whether they have open ports or not. This method can also provide information about the services and operating systems running on the discovered hosts.

Passive network discovery is another technique that can be used to discover hosts on a network. Passive network discovery involves analyzing network traffic to identify devices communicating on the network. This technique can be useful for identifying devices that are not visible to active scanning methods.

Finally, network sniffing can also be used for host discovery. Network sniffing involves capturing and analyzing network traffic to identify hosts communicating on the network. This technique can provide information about the types of traffic being transmitted on the network and the devices that are sending and receiving the traffic.

Overall, the choice of host discovery technique will depend on the specific requirements of the network and the goals of the network scanning exercise. Some techniques may be more effective than others depending on the specific network topology and devices being scanned. It is important to use a combination of techniques to ensure comprehensive host discovery and accurate network mapping.

Best Practice

Effective host discovery is critical for any network scanning or security assessment activity. Here are some best practices for conducting host discovery:

1. Use multiple host discovery techniques: No single technique can identify all the hosts on a network. Therefore, it

is important to use multiple techniques, such as ping scanning, ARP scanning, and DNS enumeration, to increase the chances of identifying all hosts on a network.

2. Customize scan parameters: Depending on the network topology and target environment, it may be necessary to customize scan parameters to optimize scan performance and avoid network congestion. This includes adjusting the number of threads used for the scan and setting timeouts and other scan parameters.

3. Conduct scans during off-peak hours: Conducting scans during off-peak hours can help reduce network congestion and minimize the impact of the scan on system performance.

4. Analyze scan results carefully: Once the scan is complete, it is important to analyze the results carefully to identify potential anomalies or errors in the scan. This may include double-checking scan results with other techniques or verifying scan results with manual validation.

5. Obtain permission: It is important to obtain permission before conducting any host discovery or network scanning activities, as unauthorized scanning can cause unnecessary harm or disruption to the network.

6. Document the scanning process: Documenting the scanning process, including the techniques used, scan parameters, and results, can help ensure that the scanning process is repeatable and consistent, and provide a basis for comparison with future scans. Additionally, documenting the process can help demonstrate compliance with relevant laws, regulations, and industry standards.

Scenarios

Scenario 1

ACME Product Company has hired an ethical hacking firm to assess the security of its network. The ethical hacking firm will conduct a host discovery process as part of its security assessment.

Step by step process:

1. Obtain necessary permissions: The first step is to obtain written permission from ACME Product Company to conduct the host discovery process. This ensures that the ethical hacking firm has legal authorization to perform the assessment.
2. Identify the scope: The ethical hacker team should determine the scope of the host discovery process. This includes identifying the IP ranges and subnets that will be scanned.
3. Choose appropriate scanning tools: The ethical hacker team should select the appropriate scanning tools for the host discovery process. Some popular tools for host discovery include Nmap, Fping, and Angry IP Scanner.
4. Configure scanning parameters: The ethical hacker team should configure the scanning parameters to ensure that the scans are conducted within the limits of the law and do not cause any unnecessary harm or disruption to the network.
5. Conduct the scans: The ethical hacker team should conduct the host discovery process using the selected scanning tools. The results of the scans should be documented

carefully and accurately, including the IP addresses and host names of identified hosts.

6. Analyze the results: The ethical hacker team should analyze the results of the host discovery process to identify any potential vulnerabilities or security risks. This includes identifying any unauthorized hosts on the network and potential entry points for attackers.

7. Document the results: The results of the host discovery process should be documented in a clear and concise report that includes recommendations for improving network security. The report should be presented to ACME Product Company along with any supporting documentation.

Suggestions for effective analysis and documentation of the results:

- Prioritize the identified hosts based on the level of risk they pose to the network.
- Provide detailed descriptions of any vulnerabilities or security risks identified during the host discovery process.
- Include recommendations for mitigating identified risks and improving overall network security.
- Use clear and concise language in the report to ensure that it is easily understood by non-technical stakeholders.
- Include any supporting documentation or screenshots to help illustrate the findings of the host discovery process.
- Use a consistent format and structure for the report to make it easy to navigate and understand.

Sample Report 1

Network Assessment Report for ACME Product Company

Overview:

ACME Product Company requested a network assessment to identify any potential vulnerabilities or weaknesses that could be exploited by malicious actors. The assessment involved conducting host discovery, port scanning, and service scanning to identify open ports and services running on the network.

Host Discovery:

The host discovery process involved using the Ping scan technique to identify active hosts on the network. This technique proved effective in identifying all active hosts on the network, including servers, printers, and workstations. No hidden or undocumented hosts were detected during the scan.

Port Scanning:

Port scanning was conducted on all active hosts identified during the host discovery process. The scan identified several open ports on the network, including Port 22 (SSH), Port 80 (HTTP), and Port 443 (HTTPS). These ports are commonly used for remote access and web services, and they pose a potential risk to the network if left unsecured.

Service Scanning:

Service scanning was conducted on all identified open ports to determine the specific services running on the network. The scan identified a vulnerable version of Apache running on Port 80, which poses a significant risk to the network. Additionally, several other services were identified on open ports, including SMB, FTP, and Telnet, which could be potentially exploited by attackers.

Recommendations:

To address the vulnerabilities identified during the assessment, ACME Product Company should take the following steps:

- Upgrade Apache to the latest version to address the identified vulnerabilities.
- Disable unnecessary services such as Telnet, FTP, and SMB to reduce the attack surface of the network.
- Implement access controls and firewall rules to limit access to critical services such as SSH.
- Conduct regular vulnerability assessments and network scans to identify and address any new vulnerabilities that may arise.

Conclusion:

Overall, the network assessment identified several potential vulnerabilities and weaknesses that could be exploited by attackers. However, by implementing the recommended actions, ACME Product Company can significantly reduce the risk of a successful attack on their network.

Scenario 2

XYZ is an online shopping company that recently detected some unusual network activity and is concerned about a possible breach. They have hired an ethical hacking firm to conduct a network scan and identify any vulnerabilities or potential entry points that could be exploited by attackers.

The ethical hacking team begins by conducting a host discovery scan using Nmap to identify all devices connected to the network. They then conduct a vulnerability assessment using Nessus and identify several potential vulnerabilities, including outdated software versions and weak passwords on some devices.

After further analysis, the ethical hacking team determines that the breach likely occurred through a phishing email that tricked an employee into clicking on a malicious link and downloading malware onto their device. This malware then spread to other devices on the network, giving the attackers access to sensitive information.

To prevent further damage, the ethical hacking team takes steps to remove the malware from all affected devices and secure the network by implementing stronger access controls and regularly updating software versions. They also recommend that the company conduct employee training on identifying and avoiding phishing emails in the future.

The ethical hacking team provides a detailed report to the company outlining their findings, including the vulnerabilities identified, the method of attack, and the steps taken to mitigate the damage and prevent future breaches. They also provide recommendations for ongoing security measures to ensure the company's network remains secure.

The ethical hacking team's thorough network scan and vulnerability assessment allowed them to identify and address potential security risks, ultimately protecting the company from further harm and demonstrating the importance of regular security assessments and employee training.

SampleReport2

Report on Vulnerability Assessment for XYZ Online Shopping Company

Introduction

This report presents the findings of a vulnerability assessment conducted for XYZ Online Shopping Company. The purpose of the assessment was to identify potential vulnerabilities in the company's network and web applications and provide recommendations for improving the security posture of the organization. The assessment was conducted from 1st April to 15th April 2023 by our ethical hacking team.

Methodology:

Our team used a combination of network scanning and web application scanning tools to identify potential vulnerabilities. We also conducted manual testing to verify the accuracy of the results obtained from the automated scanning tools. Our team followed industry-standard ethical hacking procedures and obtained prior approval from the company for conducting the assessment.

Findings:

Our assessment identified several potential vulnerabilities in the company's network and web applications. These include:

1. Outdated Software Versions: Several web applications were found to be running outdated software versions, which could be exploited by attackers to gain unauthorized access to sensitive information.
2. SQL Injection Vulnerabilities: Our team identified several instances of SQL injection vulnerabilities in the company's web applications, which could be exploited by attackers to extract sensitive information from the database.
3. Weak Passwords: Several user accounts were found to have weak passwords, which could be easily guessed or cracked by attackers.
4. Open Ports: Our network scanning tools identified several open ports that were not being used, which could be exploited by attackers to gain unauthorized access to the network.
5. Lack of Encryption: Our team found that some sensitive data was being transmitted in plain text, which could be intercepted by attackers and used for malicious purposes.

Recommendations:

To mitigate the identified vulnerabilities and improve the security posture of the organization, we recommend the following:

1. Update all web applications and software versions to their latest versions.
2. Implement input validation and parameterized queries to prevent SQL injection attacks.
3. Enforce strong password policies and implement two-

factor authentication for all user accounts.

4. Close all unused ports and implement strict access controls to prevent unauthorized access.

5. Implement encryption for all sensitive data in transit and at rest.

Conclusion:

Our assessment has identified several potential vulnerabilities in the company's network and web applications. By implementing the recommended security measures, the organization can improve its security posture and mitigate the risks associated with potential attacks. Our team is available to provide further assistance in implementing these measures and to conduct regular vulnerability assessments to ensure ongoing security.

Discussion

Host discovery is a critical component of network security assessments, and understanding the different techniques and benefits of host discovery is important for ethical hackers. Common techniques for host discovery include ping scanning, ARP scanning, and DNS enumeration. Ping scanning involves sending ICMP echo requests to network hosts, while ARP scanning involves sending ARP requests to discover hosts on a local network. DNS enumeration involves querying a DNS server to identify hosts on a network. Each technique has its own unique advantages and limitations, and ethical hackers should use a variety of techniques to maximize their results.

The benefits of conducting host discovery as part of a network security assessment include identifying potentially vulnerable hosts, detecting unauthorized devices on the network, and improving network performance by identifying and resolving network congestion issues. Ethical hackers can use host dis-covery tools like Nmap or Fing to identify devices on a network, and then compare the results to a list of authorized devices to identify any unauthorized devices.

Potential risks associated with host discovery activities in-clude causing network congestion or impact on system perfor-mance, triggering intrusion detection systems (IDS) or fire-walls, and potential legal consequences if conducted without permission. Ethical hackers should obtain permission before conducting any host discovery activities and use scanning tools that allow for customization of scan parameters.

Host discovery tools can be used to identify potential vul-nerabilities in a network by identifying network devices and analyzing the open ports and services running on those devices. In scenario 1, a combination of ping scanning and ARP scanning would be most effective for identifying potential vulnerabilities in the company's network. This would allow the ethical hacker to identify all devices on the network, including those that may not respond to ICMP requests.

Best practices for conducting effective host discovery activi-ties as part of a network security assessment include obtaining permission, using a variety of scanning techniques, scanning during off-peak hours, and analyzing the results to identify potential vulnerabilities. In scenario 2, DNS enumeration would be most effective for identifying unauthorized devices on the network. This technique would allow the ethical hacker to identify all devices registered with the company's DNS server, and then compare the results to a list of authorized devices to identify any unauthorized devices.

Host discovery tools can also be used to improve network

performance by identifying and resolving network congestion issues caused by unauthorized or misconfigured devices on the network. However, limitations of host discovery techniques include devices that may not respond to ping requests or ARP requests, and devices that are hidden behind firewalls or other security measures. These limitations can be addressed by using a variety of scanning techniques, such as DNS enumeration or port scanning, and analyzing the results to identify potential vulnerabilities.

Quiz (Solutions in Appendix)

1. What are some common techniques used for host discovery, and how do they differ from each other?
2. What are some of the benefits of conducting host discovery as part of a network security assessment?
3. How can ethical hackers use host discovery tools to identify unauthorized devices on a network?
4. What are some of the potential risks associated with conducting host discovery activities, and how can they be mitigated?
5. How can host discovery tools be used to identify potential vulnerabilities in a network?
6. In scenario 1, what host discovery technique would be most effective for identifying potential vulnerabilities in the company's network, and why?
7. What are some of the best practices for conducting effective host discovery activities as part of a network security assessment?
8. In scenario 2, what host discovery technique would be most effective for identifying unauthorized devices on the

network, and why?

9. How can host discovery tools be used to improve network performance?

10. What are some of the potential limitations of host discovery techniques, and how can they be addressed?

4

Port and Service Discovery

Port and service discovery is a critical process in network security assessments. It involves identifying the services running on a network device and the ports they are using to communicate with other devices on the network. This information can be used by ethical hackers to identify potential vulnerabilities in the network and take steps to secure the network against potential attacks.

Port scanning is the most common technique used to discover open ports and services on a network. This involves sending packets to various ports on a network device and analyzing the responses to determine which ports are open and which services are running on those ports. There are several different types of port scans that can be used, including TCP, UDP, and stealth scans.

Once the open ports and services have been identified, ethical hackers can use vulnerability scanning tools like Nessus or OpenVAS to identify potential vulnerabilities in those services. This may involve checking for known vulnerabilities or misconfigurations that could be exploited by attackers.

Another important aspect of port and service discovery is identifying unauthorized or unnecessary services that may be running on a network device. These services can be a potential point of entry for attackers and should be disabled or secured to prevent potential attacks.

In addition to port scanning, service discovery can also be accomplished using tools like banner grabbing or protocol analysis. These techniques involve analyzing the response messages sent by a network device to determine the specific services and protocols that are running on the device.

Best practices for port and service discovery include obtaining permission to conduct the scan, using a variety of scanning techniques to ensure thorough coverage, and analyzing the results to identify potential vulnerabilities. It is also important to conduct scans during off-peak hours to minimize the impact on network performance and avoid triggering intrusion detection systems (IDS) or firewalls.

Overall, port and service discovery is a critical aspect of network security assessments and should be conducted regularly to ensure the ongoing security of a network. By identifying potential vulnerabilities and taking steps to secure the network against potential attacks, ethical hackers can help organizations to protect their valuable assets and prevent data breaches.

Techniques

There are several techniques for port and service discovery. Some of the most common techniques include:

1. Port scanning: This involves scanning a range of ports on a target system to determine which ones are open and

listening for connections. Port scanning can be conducted using tools like Nmap, Masscan, or Angry IP Scanner.

2. Banner grabbing: This technique involves connecting to a port and retrieving information about the service running on that port, such as the version number or operating system. This information can be useful for identifying vulnerabilities associated with specific services.

3. Protocol detection: This involves analyzing network traffic to identify the protocols being used on a network, and the associated services running on those protocols. Tools like Wireshark can be used for protocol detection.

4. Service enumeration: This technique involves identifying services running on a target system and determining which ports those services are using. This can be done using tools like Netcat or Enum4Linux.

5. Operating system fingerprinting: This involves analyzing network traffic or connecting to a target system to identify the operating system running on that system. This information can be useful for identifying potential vulnerabilities associated with specific operating systems.

6. Web application fingerprinting: This technique involves identifying the type and version of web server software running on a target system, which can be useful for identifying potential vulnerabilities associated with specific web server software.

7. Wireless network discovery: This involves scanning for wireless networks in range and identifying the devices connected to those networks. Tools like Aircrack-ng or Kismet can be used for wireless network discovery.

8. Database discovery: This involves identifying databases running on a target system and determining the types

of databases and associated services running on those databases. Tools like SQLmap can be used for database discovery.

These techniques can be used individually or in combination to conduct a comprehensive port and service discovery scan of a target system. The choice of technique(s) used will depend on the specific goals of the scan and the information needed to conduct a thorough security assessment.

Effective port and service discovery is a critical step in network security assessments. Here are some best practices to ensure a thorough and accurate discovery process:

1. Use multiple techniques: Employing a variety of port and service discovery techniques, such as TCP and UDP scanning, banner grabbing, and application fingerprinting, can help ensure a comprehensive scan and increase the chances of identifying all open ports and services on the network.
2. Conduct scans during off-peak hours: Running port and service discovery scans during off-peak hours can help minimize the impact on network performance and reduce the risk of triggering intrusion detection or prevention systems.
3. Customize scan parameters: Scanning tools often come with default settings that may not be suitable for every network. Adjusting scan parameters, such as scan speed, port range, and timeout values, can help improve the accuracy and efficiency of the discovery process.
4. Prioritize critical systems: Identifying critical systems, such as servers or network devices, and focusing on their

ports and services can help prioritize the discovery process and ensure that critical vulnerabilities are identified and addressed first.

5. Analyze scan results: Analyzing the results of port and service discovery scans is crucial in identifying potential vulnerabilities and developing a remediation plan. It is important to thoroughly document the results, prioritize vulnerabilities based on risk, and develop a plan to address them.

6. Obtain permission: Obtaining permission before conducting port and service discovery scans is crucial in avoiding legal and ethical issues. Ensure that proper authorization is obtained from the organization's management, and that the scan is conducted within the limits of the law and the organization's policies and procedures.

Discussion

Port and service discovery is a crucial part of a network security assessment. Conducting port and service discovery can help identify potential vulnerabilities and security risks associated with specific ports and services running on network devices, as well as identify unauthorized or misconfigured services running on the network. It is essential to understand the benefits and common techniques used for port and service discovery, including TCP and UDP scanning, banner grabbing, and port knocking.

Ethical hackers can use port and service discovery tools to identify potential vulnerabilities in a network by analyzing the results and identifying potential vulnerabilities associated with specific ports and services. However, potential risks associated with port and service discovery activities include network congestion or impact on system performance, triggering intrusion detection systems (IDS) or firewalls, and potential legal consequences if conducted without permission. These risks can be mitigated by obtaining permission, conducting scans during off-peak hours, and using scanning tools that allow for customization of scan parameters.

Port and service discovery tools can be used to improve network performance by identifying and resolving network congestion issues caused by unauthorized or misconfigured services running on the network. However, it is essential to know the best practices for conducting effective port and service discovery activities, including using a variety of scanning techniques, scanning during off-peak hours, and analyzing the results to identify potential vulnerabilities.

In scenarios where the attacker has limited access to the network or is attempting to remain undetected, banner grabbing is the most effective technique for port and service discovery. However, port knocking can be used to prevent unauthorized access to a network by requiring a specific sequence of packets to be sent to a closed port before it can be opened.

Network administrators can use port and service discovery tools to identify misconfigured or unauthorized services running on the network by comparing the results to a list of authorized services to identify any unauthorized or misconfigured services running on the network. However, potential limitations of port and service discovery techniques include the use of non-standard ports, firewalls, or other security measures that may block access to certain ports or services, and false positives or negatives.

Overall, understanding the benefits, common techniques,

and potential risks and limitations associated with port and service discovery can help ensure an effective network security assessment.

Quiz (Solutions in Appendix)

1. What are the benefits of conducting port and service discovery as part of a network security assessment?
2. What are some common techniques used for port and service discovery, and how do they differ from each other?
3. How can ethical hackers use port and service discovery tools to identify potential vulnerabilities in a network?
4. What are some potential risks associated with conducting port and service discovery activities, and how can they be mitigated?
5. How can port and service discovery tools be used to improve network performance?
6. In what scenarios would banner grabbing be the most effective technique for port and service discovery, and why?
7. How can port knocking be used to prevent unauthorized access to a network?
8. What are some best practices for conducting effective port and service discovery activities as part of a network security assessment?
9. How can network administrators use port and service discovery tools to identify misconfigured or unauthorized services running on the network?
10. What are some of the potential limitations of port and service discovery techniques, and how can they be addressed?

5

OS Discovery

OS discovery is a critical component of a network security assessment. It involves identifying the specific operating systems running on network devices, which can provide valuable information about potential vulnerabilities and security issues associated with specific operating systems. There are several techniques used for OS discovery, including passive fingerprinting, active fingerprinting, and protocol analysis.

Passive fingerprinting involves analyzing network traffic to identify the specific operating systems running on network devices. This can be accomplished by analyzing network packets for specific header information or by analyzing the behavior of network devices. Passive fingerprinting is often used to identify operating systems that are configured to not respond to active fingerprinting techniques.

Active fingerprinting involves sending probes or queries to network devices to identify the specific operating system running on the device. This can be accomplished by sending specific packets to the device and analyzing the responses, or by using specialized tools like Nmap or Nessus. Active fingerprinting can be more accurate than passive fingerprinting, but it can also be more intrusive and may trigger intrusion detection systems or firewalls.

Protocol analysis involves analyzing the behavior of network devices to identify the specific operating system running on the device. This can be accomplished by analyzing the way that network devices interact with different protocols or by analyzing the way that network devices respond to specific types of traffic.

Best practices for conducting effective OS discovery activities as part of a network security assessment include obtaining permission, using a variety of techniques, analyzing the results to identify potential vulnerabilities, and taking steps to mitigate any identified vulnerabilities. It is also important to keep in mind ethical considerations, such as avoiding causing unnecessary harm or disruption to the network and ensuring that the assessment is conducted within the limits of the law.

In addition to identifying potential vulnerabilities and security issues associated with specific operating systems, OS discovery can also be used to evaluate network performance and identify potential performance issues. This can be accomplished by identifying devices running outdated or unsupported operating systems or by identifying devices that are not configured properly.

Overall, OS discovery is a critical component of any network security assessment. It provides valuable information about potential vulnerabilities and security issues associated with specific operating systems and can help network administrators and security professionals take steps to secure networks and prevent potential attacks.

Techniques

OS discovery can be accomplished through banner grabbing and OS fingerprinting techniques.

Banner grabbing involves collecting information about a device's operating system by examining the "banner" message that is sent by a device's operating system when a connection is established with a service running on that device. Banner grabbing can be performed using tools like Telnet, Netcat, or Nmap.

OS fingerprinting involves analyzing network traffic to identify specific characteristics of a device's operating system. This technique involves examining network packets and identifying unique characteristics that can be used to identify the device's operating system. OS fingerprinting can be performed using tools like Nmap or P0f.

Both techniques can provide valuable information about a device's operating system, including the version number and any known vulnerabilities associated with that version. However, banner grabbing may not always be effective, as some devices may not provide banner messages or may provide incomplete or misleading information.

OS fingerprinting may be more effective, but it can also be more time-consuming and resource-intensive. Additionally, some network security measures may block or modify network packets, which can impact the accuracy of OS fingerprinting results.

Overall, using a combination of both banner grabbing and OS fingerprinting techniques can provide the most accurate and comprehensive results for OS discovery in a network security assessment.

Banner Grabbing

Banner grabbing is a technique used to extract information about a particular service or software running on a server. This information is typically obtained from the banner message that the server sends back in response to a client request. The banner message usually contains information about the server version, operating system, and other details that can be useful for attackers or penetration testers.

Here are the step-by-step instructions for banner grabbing:

1. Identify the target server: The first step is to identify the server that you want to perform banner grabbing on. This can be done using tools like Nmap or Fping to scan the network and identify active hosts.

2. Determine the port number: Once the target server is identified, the next step is to determine the port number of the service that you want to grab the banner from. This can be done using tools like Nmap or Netcat to scan for open ports on the target server.

3. Send a request to the server: After identifying the target server and port number, the next step is to send a request to the server to retrieve the banner message. This can be done using tools like Telnet or Netcat to connect to the target server on the specified port number.

4. Analyze the banner message: Once the banner message is retrieved from the server, the next step is to analyze it to extract information about the server and the software running on it. This can be done manually by reading the banner message, or using automated tools like WhatWeb

or Wappalyzer to extract information from the banner message.

5. Document the results: After completing the banner grabbing process, it is important to document the results for future reference. This should include details about the target server, port number, and any information that was extracted from the banner message.

It is important to note that banner grabbing can be used for both legitimate purposes (such as identifying server software versions and patch levels) and for malicious purposes (such as identifying vulnerabilities or exploits). As such, it is important to obtain proper authorization and use the technique responsibly.

OS Fingerprinting

OS fingerprinting is a technique used by ethical hackers to identify the operating system (OS) running on a remote target. This is done by analyzing the responses to packets sent to the target and comparing them to known responses from different operating systems. Here are the steps involved in OS fingerprinting:

1. Choose an OS fingerprinting tool: There are several OS fingerprinting tools available, such as Nmap, pOf, and Xprobe2. Choose the tool that best suits your needs and capabilities.

2. Scan the target: Use the tool to send packets to the target and capture the responses. This can be done in a variety of ways, including sending TCP or UDP packets to specific

ports.

3. Analyze the responses: Once you have captured the responses, analyze them to identify patterns or characteristics that can be used to identify the operating system. This
can include information such as the TCP/IP stack used, the
size of the window, and the TTL (Time to Live) value.

4. Compare the responses: Compare the responses you have
captured to known responses from different operating
systems. This can be done manually or with the help of a
tool that automates the comparison process.

5. Determine the operating system: Based on the analysis and
comparison of the responses, determine the most likely
operating system running on the target.

6. Verify the results: Once you have identified the operating
system, verify your results by conducting further tests or
by comparing them to other sources of information.

7. Document your findings: Document your findings in a
report that includes details about the OS fingerprinting tool
used, the scanning methodology, and the results obtained.
It is also important to include any potential limitations or
caveats in your findings.

Overall, OS fingerprinting can be a valuable technique for ethical
hackers to identify potential vulnerabilities and security risks
associated with specific operating systems running on network
devices. However, it is important to obtain permission and
use caution when conducting these types of activities to avoid
causing harm or disruption to the network.

Tools

Banner grabbing is a technique used to gather information about a specific service running on a particular port by collecting its banner or response message. There are several tools available for banner grabbing, including:

1. Netcat - a command-line utility that can be used to establish connections to specific ports and collect banner information. Netcat is available for download on the official website for free: https://netcat.sourceforge.io/
2. Telnet - a client-server protocol used to establish connections to remote systems. Telnet can be used to connect to specific ports and collect banner information. Telnet is included in most operating systems, including Windows and Linux.
3. BannerGrab - a Python-based tool that can be used to automate banner grabbing. BannerGrab is available for download on the official GitHub page: https://github.com/viperbluff/BannerGrab
4. Nmap - a popular network exploration and security auditing tool that can be used to perform banner grabbing. Nmap is available for download on the official website: https://nmap.org/download.html

OS fingerprinting is a technique used to determine the operating system running on a target device by analyzing the responses to specific network packets. Some of the popular tools used for OS fingerprinting include:

1. Nmap - as well as being used for banner grabbing, Nmap

can also be used for OS fingerprinting. Nmap uses a variety of techniques to identify the operating system running on a target device, including TCP/IP stack fingerprinting, network distance measurement, and comparison of open ports and services. Nmap is available for download on the official website: https://nmap.org/download.html

2. P0f - a passive OS fingerprinting tool that analyzes network traffic to identify the operating system running on a target device. P0f is available for download on the official website: http://lcamtuf.coredump.cx/p0f3/

3. Xprobe - an active OS fingerprinting tool that sends a series of specially crafted packets to a target device to identify the operating system running on the device. Xprobe is available for download on the official website: https://sourceforge.net/projects/xprobe/

4. Nmap Scripting Engine - Nmap also includes a scripting engine that can be used to write custom scripts for OS fingerprinting. The Nmap Scripting Engine is included in the Nmap download.

It is important to note that while these tools can be useful for banner grabbing and OS fingerprinting, they should only be used for legal and ethical purposes, and with the permission of the owner of the target system.

Telnet

It is not recommended to use Telnet as it is an unsecured protocol and passwords can be easily intercepted. Instead, it is recommended to use SSH, which provides secure encrypted communications.

However, if you still need to activate Telnet on a Windows Server, here are the step-by-step instructions:

1. Open the Start menu and search for "Programs and Features" and select it from the list of results.
2. Click on the "Turn Windows features on or off" link in the left-hand menu.
3. Scroll down and find the "Telnet Client" option and check the box next to it.
4. Click on "OK" to save the changes.
5. Wait for the installation process to complete. Once complete, you should be able to use the Telnet client to connect to a Telnet server.

Please note that it is important to consider the security risks of using Telnet and implement appropriate measures to secure your network.

Best Practice

Effective OS discovery is an important aspect of network security assessments. Here are some best practices to follow when conducting OS discovery:

1. Obtain permission: Always obtain permission from the network owner or administrator before conducting OS discovery activities. Unauthorized access to a network can result in legal consequences.
2. Use a variety of techniques: Different techniques may be more effective for discovering the OS of different types of devices. For example, banner grabbing may be more

effective for identifying the OS of a web server, while OS fingerprinting may be more effective for identifying the OS of a router. Using a variety of techniques can increase the chances of identifying the OS of all devices on the network.

3. Use reliable tools: Use reliable OS discovery tools that are well-documented and have a proven track record of accuracy. Tools like Nmap, Netcat, and Hping3 are commonly used for OS discovery.

4. Customize scans: Customize scans to focus on specific devices or ranges of IP addresses. This can help reduce the impact of scans on network performance and reduce the likelihood of triggering intrusion detection systems.

5. Analyze results: Thoroughly analyze the results of OS discovery scans to identify potential vulnerabilities and security risks associated with specific operating systems. This information can be used to develop a plan for securing the network.

6. Keep documentation: Keep documentation of OS discovery activities, including the tools used, scan parameters, and results. This documentation can be used for future reference and to demonstrate compliance with security standards.

By following these best practices, ethical hackers can conduct effective OS discovery activities as part of a comprehensive network security assessment.

Discussion

OS discovery is the process of identifying the operating system running on network devices, which is crucial in a network security assessment to identify potential vulnerabilities and security risks associated with specific operating systems. Common techniques used for OS discovery include banner grabbing, operating system fingerprinting, and protocol analysis. Banner grabbing involves analyzing the banner message sent by network services to identify the operating system running on the device. Operating system fingerprinting involves analyzing network packets and responses to identify the specific operating system running on the device. Protocol analysis involves analyzing network protocols to identify the specific operating system running on the device.

The benefits of using banner grabbing for OS discovery include simplicity and speed, while limitations include the potential for false positives and the reliance on the accuracy of the banner message sent by the network service. In contrast, the benefits of using operating system fingerprinting for OS discovery include greater accuracy and the ability to detect operating system versions, while limitations include the potential for false negatives and the need for more sophisticated tools.

Ethical hackers can use OS discovery tools like Nmap or Amap to identify the specific operating system running on target devices, which can provide valuable information about potential vulnerabilities and security issues associated with specific operating systems. However, potential risks associated with OS discovery activities include causing network congestion or impact on system performance, triggering intrusion detection systems (IDS) or firewalls, and potential legal consequences if conducted without permission. These risks can be mitigated by obtaining permission, conducting scans during off-peak hours, and using scanning tools that allow for customization of scan parameters.

Network administrators can use OS discovery tools to improve network security and performance by identifying potential vulnerabilities associated with specific operating systems and implementing security measures to address them. They can also use OS discovery tools to identify misconfigured or outdated systems that may be impacting network performance. Best practices for conducting effective OS discovery activities include obtaining permission, using a variety of scanning techniques, scanning during off-peak hours, and analyzing the results to identify potential vulnerabilities.

The use of honeypots and decoys can improve the effectiveness of OS discovery activities by diverting attackers away from critical network resources and providing false information about the network to discourage further attacks. Potential limitations of OS discovery techniques include the use of obfuscation techniques to hide the true operating system, the presence of virtualized or containerized environments that may appear as different operating systems, and the need for advanced tools to accurately identify the operating system. These limitations can be addressed by using a variety of scanning techniques and analyzing the results to identify potential vulnerabilities.

Quiz (Solutions in Appendix)

1. What is OS discovery and why is it important in a network security assessment?
2. What are some common techniques used for OS discovery,

and how do they differ from each other?

3. What are the benefits and limitations of using banner grabbing for OS discovery?

4. What are the benefits and limitations of using operating system fingerprinting for OS discovery?

5. How can ethical hackers use OS discovery tools to identify potential vulnerabilities in a network?

6. What are some potential risks associated with conducting OS discovery activities, and how can they be mitigated?

7. How can network administrators use OS discovery tools to improve network security and performance?

8. What are some best practices for conducting effective OS discovery activities as part of a network security assessment?

9. How can the use of honeypots and decoys improve the effectiveness of OS discovery activities?

10. What are some potential limitations of OS discovery techniques, and how can they be addressed?

6

Scanning Beyond IDS and Firewall

In Chapter 6, we will discuss scanning beyond intrusion detection systems (IDS) and firewalls, which are commonly used to protect networks from external attacks. While IDS and firewalls are important components of network security, they may not always be effective in detecting and preventing advanced threats. Scanning beyond these tools involves using more advanced scanning techniques to identify potential vulnerabilities and security risks in a network.

One common technique for scanning beyond IDS and firewalls is port scanning. This involves sending packets to target ports on a network device to determine if they are open or closed. Port scanning can help identify open ports that may be vulnerable to attack.

Another technique for scanning beyond IDS and firewalls is vulnerability scanning. This involves using automated tools to scan network devices for known vulnerabilities, which can help identify potential security risks that may be missed by traditional security tools.

In addition to port and vulnerability scanning, other techniques for scanning beyond IDS and firewalls include banner grabbing, operating system fingerprinting, and protocol analysis. These techniques can help identify specific operating systems and network protocols running on network devices, which can provide valuable information about potential vulnerabilities and security risks.

Limitations of IDS and Firewall

In the context of network security, intrusion detection systems (IDS) and firewalls are two essential components that help protect networks from cyber-attacks. While both systems are designed to monitor network traffic and prevent unauthorized access, they have limitations that can be exploited by attackers.

IDS is a passive security measure that monitors network traffic for known attack patterns and generates alerts when it detects such patterns. However, IDS has several limitations. Firstly, it can only detect known attack patterns, and it is not effective against zero-day attacks or unknown threats. Secondly, IDS can generate a high number of false positives, which can be time-consuming to investigate and may result in ignoring legitimate alerts.

On the other hand, firewalls are a proactive security measure that acts as a barrier between the internet and the local network, allowing only authorized traffic to pass through. However, firewalls have limitations as well. Firstly, firewalls can be bypassed by attackers who use legitimate network protocols or encrypted traffic to evade detection. Secondly, firewalls are not effective against insider threats, which are attacks carried out by employees or contractors with authorized access to the network.

Therefore, it is essential to have additional security measures in place to complement IDS and firewalls, such as network scanning techniques that go beyond IDS and firewall detection capabilities. These scanning techniques can help identify vulnerabilities and potential threats that IDS and firewalls may miss. However, it is important to note that these scanning techniques can also have limitations and risks, such as causing network congestion, triggering IDS or firewall alerts, and legal consequences if conducted without permission. It is crucial to follow best practices and obtain permission before conducting any network scanning activities.

Weaknesses of IDS and Firewalls

Here are some weaknesses of IDS and firewalls:

1. False positives: IDS and firewalls can generate false alarms, which can be a nuisance to network administrators and distract them from actual security events.
2. False negatives: IDS and firewalls can also miss actual security events, leaving the network vulnerable to attacks.
3. Encrypted traffic: IDS and firewalls may not be able to inspect encrypted traffic, making it difficult to detect threats that are hidden within encrypted traffic.
4. Malware evasion: Sophisticated malware can be designed to evade detection by IDS and firewalls by using techniques such as polymorphism, obfuscation, and encryption.
5. Zero-day attacks: IDS and firewalls may not be able to detect zero-day attacks, which are attacks that exploit vulnerabilities that are not yet known or patched.
6. Misconfiguration: Misconfiguration of IDS and firewalls

can create vulnerabilities that can be exploited by attackers.

7. Over-reliance: Over-reliance on IDS and firewalls can lead
   to a false sense of security and neglect of other important
   security measures.

8. Cost: IDS and firewalls can be expensive to implement and
   maintain, making them unaffordable for some organizations.

9. Complexity: IDS and firewalls can be complex to configure
   and manage, requiring specialized knowledge and skills.

10. Human error: Human error, such as misconfigurations or
    failure to update security policies, can create vulnerabili-
    ties that can be exploited by attackers.

Techniques for Bypassing IDS and Firewall

Packet Fragmentation

Packet fragmentation refers to the process of breaking a packet
into smaller fragments to enable its transmission over a network
that imposes a maximum packet size. This technique can be
used to bypass network security measures such as IDS and
firewalls that may be configured to inspect only the first packet
in a series.

One of the primary risks associated with packet fragmentation
is the potential for the fragments to be reassembled in a way
that is different from the original packet. This can result in
packet loss or duplication, and can even cause the packet to be
discarded entirely.

To prevent these issues, network administrators can use
tools like packet analyzers to inspect packet fragmentation

and reassembly in real-time. They can also implement best practices such as setting maximum transmission unit (MTU) limits, enabling IP fragmentation filtering, and configuring routers to prevent fragmentation.

However, attackers may still attempt to exploit packet fragmentation by using techniques such as overlapping fragments or intentionally malformed packets. To mitigate these risks, network administrators can implement intrusion prevention systems (IPS) that are designed to detect and block such attacks.

Overall, packet fragmentation is an important technique for network communication, but it must be used with caution to prevent potential security risks.

Protocol manipulation

Protocol manipulation is a technique used by attackers to bypass IDS and firewalls. It involves altering the headers of network packets to change the characteristics of the traffic, making it difficult for security systems to identify and block the malicious traffic. Attackers can manipulate protocols in a variety of ways, including:

1. Changing the protocol type: Attackers can alter the protocol type of a packet to bypass security controls that are configured to monitor specific protocols. For example, an attacker might change an HTTP packet to a TCP packet to evade detection.

2. Modifying protocol headers: Attackers can modify protocol headers to change the characteristics of network traffic, making it more difficult for security systems to identify malicious activity. For example, an attacker might modify

the TCP header to change the source or destination port, making it more difficult for a firewall to identify the traffic.

3. Using tunneling protocols: Attackers can use tunneling protocols to encapsulate malicious traffic within a legitimate protocol, making it more difficult for security systems to identify the malicious activity. For example, an attacker might use the SSH protocol to create an encrypted tunnel to send malicious traffic through a network undetected.

Traffic encryption and tunneling

Traffic encryption and tunneling can be used to bypass security measures such as IDS and firewalls because they allow for the concealment of traffic and can create a secure communication channel between two endpoints. By encrypting traffic, attackers can prevent it from being read or intercepted by security devices that rely on inspecting traffic contents to detect and block malicious activity.

Tunneling can be used to encapsulate traffic within another protocol, making it appear as benign traffic to security devices. For example, an attacker could use a technique like Secure Shell (SSH) tunneling to create an encrypted channel between two endpoints and encapsulate malicious traffic within the encrypted channel, effectively bypassing any security devices that are not configured to inspect encrypted traffic.

Similarly, traffic encryption can be used to prevent traffic from being inspected or blocked by security devices. For example, attackers could use Secure Sockets Layer (SSL) encryption to encrypt traffic between endpoints, preventing it from being inspected or blocked by security devices that rely on inspecting traffic contents.

While traffic encryption and tunneling can be used to bypass security measures, they can also be used for legitimate purposes, such as secure remote access to corporate networks. However, it is important for security professionals to be aware of these techniques and implement appropriate measures to detect and block malicious activity that may be using them.

Techniques for preventing bypass of IDS and Firewall

There are several techniques that can be implemented to prevent bypass of IDS and firewall:

1. Implement a multi-layered security approach: This involves implementing multiple layers of security such as network segmentation, intrusion prevention systems, and security information and event management (SIEM) systems. This ensures that even if one layer of security is bypassed, there are other layers in place to prevent an attack.

2. Keep IDS and firewall updated: Keeping the IDS and firewall updated with the latest signatures and patches can help prevent new and emerging threats.

3. Implement strong authentication and access controls: Strong authentication methods such as two-factor authentication and strong password policies can help prevent unauthorized access to the network.

4. Implement encryption: Encryption can prevent attackers from intercepting and deciphering sensitive data as it is transmitted across the network.

5. Monitor network traffic: Regularly monitoring network

traffic can help identify anomalous behavior that may indicate a potential attack. This can include setting up alerts for unusual traffic patterns or unusual activity on specific ports.

6. Conduct regular vulnerability assessments and penetration testing: Regular vulnerability assessments and penetration testing can help identify potential vulnerabilities in the network and allow for timely mitigation.

7. Implement intrusion prevention and detection systems: Intrusion prevention and detection systems can detect and prevent attacks by blocking traffic that matches known attack signatures.

8. Implement firewall rules and policies: Implementing firewall rules and policies can prevent unauthorized access to the network by blocking traffic that does not meet specific criteria.

9. Use honeypots: Honeypots can be used to attract attackers and divert them away from critical systems and data.

10. Implement network segmentation: Network segmentation can help prevent lateral movement by isolating different parts of the network and restricting access between them.

To prevent protocol manipulation, organizations should consider implementing the following best practices:

1. Implement protocol-specific security controls: Organizations should implement security controls that are specific to the protocols used in their network. For example, if an organization primarily uses HTTP traffic, they should consider implementing a web application firewall (WAF) to monitor and block malicious traffic.

2. Conduct regular protocol analysis: Regular protocol analysis can help organizations identify and block traffic that deviates from expected protocol behavior. Network administrators can use tools like Wireshark or tcpdump to monitor and analyze network traffic.

3. Use encrypted traffic inspection: Encrypted traffic inspection can help organizations detect and block malicious traffic that is using encryption to evade detection. Organizations can use tools like SSL/TLS decryption tools to inspect encrypted traffic for signs of malicious activity.

4. Keep security systems up to date: Organizations should ensure that their security systems are up to date with the latest software patches and security updates. This can help ensure that security systems are capable of identifying and blocking the latest threats, including those that use protocol manipulation.

Best Practices

Best practices for effective scanning beyond IDS and Firewall include:

1. Obtaining proper authorization: It is important to obtain proper authorization before conducting any scanning activity beyond IDS and firewall to ensure that the assessment is conducted within legal and ethical boundaries.

2. Selecting the right tools: Choosing the right tools for the task is essential for successful scanning beyond IDS and firewall. Some popular tools for network scanning include Nmap, Hping, and ZMap.

3. Understanding the network topology: Understanding the

network topology is crucial for effective scanning beyond IDS and firewall. Network topology mapping tools such as NetTopologySuite and Visio can help in creating network topology maps.

4. Using stealth techniques: Using stealth techniques can help prevent detection and increase the success rate of scanning beyond IDS and firewall. Techniques such as port knocking and tunneling can be effective in bypassing firewall and IDS.

5. Conducting regular scans: Regular scanning beyond IDS and firewall can help identify new vulnerabilities and security risks that may arise due to changes in the network environment. It is recommended to conduct scans at regular intervals such as monthly or quarterly.

6. Keeping logs and documentation: Keeping detailed logs and documentation of scanning activities can help track progress, identify trends, and provide an audit trail for future reference. Tools such as Metasploit and Nessus provide a mechanism for generating reports and logs.

7. Identifying and mitigating risks: After conducting scanning beyond IDS and firewall, it is important to identify and mitigate any vulnerabilities or security risks that are discovered. This may include patching systems, configuring firewalls, or updating intrusion prevention systems.

Overall, effective scanning beyond IDS and firewall requires careful planning, proper authorization, and the use of appropriate tools and techniques. It is important to prioritize security and follow best practices to ensure the integrity and confidentiality of network assets.

Discussion

It is important for network security assessments to consider the limitations of intrusion detection systems (IDS) and firewalls in detecting and preventing network attacks. These security measures can be limited in their ability to detect sophisticated attacks that use evasion techniques or disguise themselves as legitimate traffic. Additionally, they may fail to detect attacks executed within the perimeter of the network. As a result, ethical hackers may need to employ more advanced techniques to identify potential vulnerabilities.

Common techniques used for bypassing IDS and firewalls include packet fragmentation, protocol manipulation, traffic encryption, and tunneling. By fragmenting packets, an attacker can send malicious traffic in smaller pieces that are more difficult to detect. Protocol manipulation involves altering the content of network traffic to evade detection, while traffic encryption and tunneling allow attackers to hide malicious traffic within encrypted or tunneled traffic that may not be monitored by IDS or firewalls.

Vulnerability scanners are an effective tool for identifying potential vulnerabilities on a network, but they may also produce false positives and require periodic updates to vulnerability databases. Best practices for conducting effective vulnerability scans include obtaining permission, using up-to-date scanning tools, conducting scans during off-peak hours, and analyzing the results to identify potential vulnerabilities.

Social engineering techniques such as phishing or pretexting can be used by ethical hackers to bypass network security measures. By tricking users into divulging sensitive information or granting access to restricted areas of the network, an attacker can gain access to the network.

Intrusion prevention systems (IPS) can be configured to detect and block network attacks in real-time using predefined signatures and heuristics to identify suspicious network activity. However, they also have limitations and may not be effective against sophisticated attacks that use advanced techniques to bypass security measures.

Honeypots and decoys can be used as part of a network security strategy to divert attackers away from critical network assets and provide false information about the network. However, if not properly managed, they can divert valuable resources away from critical network assets and provide a false sense of security.

Common techniques for obfuscating network traffic include encryption, tunneling, steganography, and traffic shaping. By encrypting or tunneling malicious traffic, an attacker can hide it within seemingly legitimate traffic that may not be monitored by IDS or firewalls.

To protect against sophisticated attacks that bypass traditional security measures, network administrators can use a layered approach to network security. This approach involves using multiple security measures, such as firewalls, IDS, IPS, vulnerability scanners, and access controls, to detect and prevent network attacks. By using multiple security measures, network administrators can increase the chances of detecting and preventing potential vulnerabilities and security risks associated with the network.

Quiz (Solutions in Appendix)

1. What are some of the limitations of intrusion detection systems (IDS) and firewalls in detecting and preventing network attacks?
2. What are some common techniques used for bypassing IDS and firewalls?
3. How can ethical hackers use port scanning tools to identify open ports and services on a network?
4. What are the benefits and limitations of using vulnerability scanners as part of a network security assessment?
5. What are some best practices for conducting effective vulnerability scans as part of a network security assessment?
6. How can ethical hackers use social engineering techniques to bypass network security measures?
7. How can network administrators use intrusion prevention systems (IPS) to detect and prevent network attacks?
8. What are some of the potential risks associated with using honeypots and decoys as part of a network security strategy?
9. What are some common techniques used for obfuscating network traffic to bypass IDS and firewalls?
10. How can network administrators use a layered approach to network security to protect against sophisticated attacks that bypass traditional security measures?

7

Draw Network Diagrams

Network diagrams are important tools used in network management and administration. A network diagram is a visual representation of the components of a network, including devices
such as routers, switches, firewalls, servers, and workstations,
and the connections between them. These diagrams provide a
clear and concise way of understanding the network's layout,
which can be helpful in identifying and troubleshooting network
issues, planning for network expansions or upgrades, and
providing documentation for network administrators.

Without a network diagram, network administrators can
struggle to understand the network topology, which can make
it difficult to effectively manage and maintain the network.
This lack of understanding can lead to inefficient use of network resources, slow network performance, and increased
vulnerability to security breaches. Additionally, without a clear
and concise understanding of the network topology, network
administrators may find it difficult to plan for future network
changes or expansions.

Network diagrams are also helpful in communicating the

network layout to other stakeholders, including upper management and external contractors. This visual representation can help stakeholders understand the network's complexity and the implications of changes made to the network.

Overall, network diagrams are an important tool for network administrators in managing and maintaining their networks. By providing a clear and concise understanding of the network topology, network diagrams can help identify and troubleshoot network issues, plan for future changes, and communicate the network layout to other stakeholders.

Techniques

The following are some techniques for drawing network diagrams:

1. Identify the scope of the network: The first step in drawing a network diagram is to identify the scope of the network, including the number of devices, their locations, and the connections between them.
2. Choose a diagramming tool: There are many diagramming tools available, such as Microsoft Visio, Lucidchart, and Draw.io. Choose a tool that meets your needs and has the features required to accurately represent your network.
3. Determine the layout: Once you have identified the scope of the network and chosen a diagramming tool, determine the layout of the network diagram. This may involve choosing a specific orientation, such as top-down or left-to-right, and deciding on the level of detail to include.
4. Add network devices: Add network devices to the diagram, including routers, switches, firewalls, servers, worksta-

tions, printers, and other devices.

5. Add connections: Add connections between network devices, including LAN and WAN connections, VPN connections, and wireless connections.

6. Label devices and connections: Label each device and connection on the network diagram with a descriptive name, IP address, and other relevant information.

7. Organize the diagram: Organize the network diagram in a logical and easy-to-understand manner, such as by grouping devices by location or function.

8. Review and revise: Once the network diagram is complete, review it carefully and revise as needed to ensure accuracy and completeness.

9. Share the diagram: Share the network diagram with other members of the IT team, network administrators, or other stakeholders as needed.

10. Update the diagram: Keep the network diagram up to date by revising it as changes are made to the network, such as new devices or connections being added or Removed.

Best Practices

Best practices for effective network diagrams include:

1. Use standard symbols and labels: Standard symbols and labels make it easier for others to understand the diagram and ensure consistency across different diagrams.

2. Keep it simple: A clear and concise diagram is easier to understand and maintain. Avoid cluttering the diagram with unnecessary information or details.

3. Label everything: Every device, connection, and compo-

nent should be labeled in the diagram to ensure accuracy and clarity.

4. Use color coding: Color coding can help distinguish different components or types of connections, making it easier to understand the diagram.

5. Keep it up-to-date: Network diagrams should be updated regularly to reflect changes in the network topology or configuration.

6. Use a consistent layout: A consistent layout can make it easier to compare different network diagrams and ensure that important information is always located in the same place.

7. Include a legend: A legend or key can help others understand the meaning of different symbols and labels used in the diagram.

8. Document the purpose of the diagram: Include a brief description of the purpose of the diagram, such as troubleshooting or network planning.

9. Use tools to automate the process: Tools like Microsoft Visio, Lucidchart, and draw.io can simplify the process of creating and maintaining network diagrams.

10. Share the diagram with relevant stakeholders: Network diagrams should be shared with relevant stakeholders, such as network administrators or security personnel, to ensure everyone has a clear understanding of the network topology and configuration.

Discussion

The purpose of creating a network diagram is to provide a visual representation of the network infrastructure, which helps in identifying potential vulnerabilities, mapping network traffic flows, and improving network management. Network diagrams can be created using a variety of tools and techniques, including pen and paper, Microsoft Visio, Lucidchart, and network mapping software. Best practices for creating effective network diagrams include using standardized symbols and labels, updating the diagrams regularly, including all relevant network components, and keeping the diagrams organized and easily accessible.

Network diagrams can be used to identify potential security risks and vulnerabilities in a network by mapping network traffic flows, identifying single points of failure, and identifying network components that are not properly secured. Common challenges when creating network diagrams include incomplete or outdated information, difficulty in identifying all network components, and the need to update the diagrams regularly. These challenges can be addressed by using automated network mapping tools, working closely with network administrators, and conducting regular reviews of the diagrams.

Network diagrams can be used to improve network performance and management by providing a clear overview of the network infrastructure, identifying bottlenecks and other performance issues, and facilitating efficient network management. Potential risks associated with creating and sharing network diagrams include the risk of unauthorized access to sensitive network information and the risk of inadvertently exposing vulnerabilities. These risks can be mitigated by restricting access to the diagrams, encrypting sensitive information, and properly disposing of outdated diagrams.

Network diagrams can be used to ensure compliance with industry regulations and standards by providing a clear overview of the network infrastructure, identifying areas that are not compliant with the standards, and facilitating the implementation of required security measures. Network diagrams can also be used to support incident response and disaster recovery efforts by providing a clear overview of the network infrastructure, identifying critical network components and dependencies, and facilitating efficient restoration of services in the event of a network outage.

Overall, network diagrams can be a valuable tool for network security assessments, as they provide a standardized and easily understandable representation of the network infrastructure. They can be used to identify potential vulnerabilities, support incident response and disaster recovery efforts, and improve communication and collaboration between different stakeholders in a network security assessment.

Quiz (Solutions in Appendix)

1. What is the purpose of creating a network diagram, and how does it help in a network security assessment?
2. What are some common tools and techniques used for drawing network diagrams, and how do they differ from each other?
3. What are some best practices for creating effective network diagrams as part of a network security assessment?
4. How can network diagrams be used to identify potential security risks and vulnerabilities in a network?

5. What are some common challenges that may arise when creating network diagrams, and how can they be addressed?
6. How can network diagrams be used to improve network performance and management?
7. What are some potential risks associated with creating and sharing network diagrams, and how can they be mitigated?
8. How can network diagrams be used to ensure compliance with industry regulations and standards?
9. How can network diagrams be used to support incident response and disaster recovery efforts?
10. How can network diagrams be used to improve communication and collaboration between different stakeholders in a network security assessment?

8

Network Scanning in Action

Network scanning is a crucial aspect of network security assessments and is used to identify potential vulnerabilities and security risks in a network. In this chapter, we will explore network scanning in action through the analysis of three real-life case studies.

The first case study will examine the Target breach, which occurred in 2013 and resulted in the theft of 40 million credit and debit card numbers. The attackers used network scanning tools to identify vulnerabilities in Target's network and gain access to their systems.

The second case study will focus on the WannaCry ransomware attack that occurred in 2017 and impacted organizations worldwide. The attack used network scanning tools to identify vulnerable systems and exploit a known vulnerability in the Windows operating system.

Finally, we will discuss the SolarWinds supply chain attack that was discovered in 2020 and impacted multiple US government agencies and organizations. The attackers used network scanning tools to infiltrate the SolarWinds network and gain access to their software updates, which were then used to distribute malicious software to their customers.

By examining these case studies, we will gain a deeper under-standing of the importance of network scanning in identifying potential vulnerabilities and security risks in a network and the devastating impact that can occur if these risks are not properly addressed.

The Target Breach

The Target breach is one of the most notable examples of a network security breach resulting from the use of scanning tools. Attackers were able to steal the credit and debit card information of approximately 40 million Target customers, as well as the personal information of 70 million customers, in what is considered to be one of the largest data breaches in history.

The attackers gained access to Target's network through the use of a vulnerability scanner, which was used to identify weaknesses in the network's perimeter defenses. Specifically, the attackers were able to exploit a vulnerability in Target's payment card system, which allowed them to gain access to the company's internal network.

Once inside the network, the attackers used a range of scan-ning tools to locate and exploit further vulnerabilities. They used a tool called "Responder" to intercept network traffic and steal login credentials, as well as a tool called "Metasploit" to exploit a vulnerability in a web application and gain access to Target's point-of-sale (POS) system.

The attackers were also able to use a network scanning tool called "Nmap" to map the Target network and identify additional vulnerabilities. They used this information to move laterally across the network and access other systems and data.

The Target breach highlights the importance of effective network scanning and vulnerability management. Had Target implemented more robust perimeter defenses and had a more effective vulnerability management program in place, it is possible that the breach could have been prevented or mitigated. It also demonstrates the need for organizations to be vigilant in monitoring their networks for suspicious activity and responding promptly to potential security incidents.

WannaCry ransomware attack

The WannaCry ransomware attack was a global cyberattack that occurred in May 2017, which affected over 200,000 computers in 150 countries. The attack exploited a vulnerability in Microsoft Windows operating systems, using a tool called EternalBlue, which was developed by the National Security Agency (NSA) and later leaked by a hacking group called the Shadow Brokers.

The attackers used network scanning tools to identify vulnerable systems with unpatched versions of Windows, which allowed the ransomware to propagate rapidly across networks. Once a computer was infected, the ransomware encrypted the files on the system and displayed a message demanding payment in exchange for the decryption key.

The attack impacted a wide range of organizations, including hospitals, government agencies, and businesses. The total cost of the attack was estimated to be in the billions of dollars, with many organizations experiencing significant downtime and loss of data.

The use of network scanning tools was critical in the WannaCry attack, as it allowed the attackers to quickly identify and exploit vulnerable systems. In response to the attack, organizations were urged to ensure that their systems were up-to-date with the latest security patches and to implement strong network security measures to prevent similar attacks in the future. The attack highlighted the importance of proactive security measures, including regular vulnerability scans and patch management to prevent exploitation of known vulnerabilities.

SolarWinds Supply Chain Attack

The SolarWinds supply chain attack was a cyberattack that occurred in December 2020 and affected numerous organizations worldwide. The attack was executed by exploiting vulnerabilities in SolarWinds' Orion network management software, which allowed the attackers to gain access to sensitive information and carry out espionage activities. The attackers were believed to be associated with a Russian state-sponsored hacking group known as APT29 or Cozy Bear.

The attackers used a variety of techniques to bypass network security measures and remain undetected, including the use of network scanning tools. They conducted extensive reconnaissance activities to identify potential targets and carried out network scans to identify vulnerabilities in the target systems. They then used the vulnerabilities to gain access to the systems and implant malware that allowed them to exfiltrate data and carry out further attacks.

The attackers used a modified version of the SolarWinds Orion software, which contained a backdoor that allowed them to gain access to the targeted systems. The backdoor was designed to blend in with legitimate traffic and was difficult to detect. The attackers also used techniques such as domain fronting and IP masquerading to hide their activities and evade detection.

The SolarWinds supply chain attack highlights the importance of network security and the need for effective network scanning tools and techniques. It also underscores the need for organizations to take proactive measures to prevent and detect cyberattacks, including implementing network segmentation, conducting regular vulnerability assessments and penetration testing, and using tools such as intrusion detection and prevention systems (IDS/IPS) and endpoint detection and response (EDR) systems.

Best Practices

Here are some best practices for using network scanning for network security:

1. Obtain permission: Always obtain permission before conducting any network scanning activities to avoid violating any laws or regulations.
2. Use updated tools: Use up-to-date network scanning tools to ensure accurate and reliable results.
3. Use multiple scanning techniques: Use a combination of scanning techniques, such as port scanning, vulnerability scanning, and penetration testing, to identify potential vulnerabilities and attack vectors.
4. Use secure protocols: Use secure protocols, such as SSL/TLS, to prevent network traffic from being intercepted or compromised during scanning activities.
5. Conduct scans during off-peak hours: Schedule scans

during off-peak hours to minimize network impact and prevent disruptions to normal network activities.

6. Analyze and prioritize results: Analyze and prioritize scan results based on the severity of vulnerabilities, the criticality of network components, and the level of risk to the organization.

7. Follow up on identified vulnerabilities: Follow up on identified vulnerabilities by implementing appropriate security measures and verifying their effectiveness.

8. Regularly update and review network diagrams: Regularly update and review network diagrams to ensure accurate and up-to-date representations of the network infrastructure.

9. Keep logs and documentation: Keep logs and documentation of all scanning activities, including the tools used, the scan parameters, and the results obtained, for future reference and analysis.

10. Maintain confidentiality: Maintain confidentiality of all scanning activities and results to prevent sensitive information from being exposed or misused.

Discussion

The Target breach exploited vulnerabilities in the company's payment systems and network segmentation, allowing the attackers to move laterally across the network and steal sensitive data. Network scanning tools could have been used to identify weaknesses in the network segmentation and detect any suspicious network activity that may have indicated a potential attack.

The WannaCry ransomware attack used network scanning

tools to identify vulnerable systems running outdated software and exploited these vulnerabilities to propagate across networks. The attack highlights the importance of keeping software up to date and using network scanning tools to detect vulnerabilities and potential security risks.

In the SolarWinds supply chain attack, network scanning tools were used to identify vulnerable systems and deliver the malware through software updates. The main targets were government agencies and companies that used SolarWinds' network management software.

Best practices for using network scanning tools include conducting regular scans to identify potential vulnerabilities, using up-to-date scanning tools, analyzing scan results to prioritize vulnerabilities, and implementing security measures to address identified risks.

Network scanning tools can be used to identify bottlenecks and other performance issues in the network, as well as to track network activity and monitor network performance over time. This information can be used to optimize network configurations and improve overall network management.

Ethical hackers can use network scanning tools to identify potential vulnerabilities and security risks in a network, including open ports, weak passwords, and outdated software. This information can be used to recommend and implement security measures to prevent malicious attacks.

Potential risks associated with using network scanning tools include triggering intrusion detection systems or firewalls, causing network congestion or impact on system performance, and potentially exposing sensitive information if not properly secured. These risks can be mitigated by using customized scan parameters, scanning during off-peak hours, and implementing proper access controls and encryption measures.

Network scanning tools can be used to identify areas of the network that are not compliant with industry regulations and standards, such as weak passwords or outdated software. This information can be used to implement required security measures and ensure compliance with regulations and standards.

Limitations of network scanning tools can include false positives, incomplete or outdated information, and the need for periodic updates to scanning databases. These limitations can be addressed by using a variety of scanning techniques, verifying scan results with additional testing, and keeping scanning tools and databases up to date.

A potential limitation of relying solely on network scanning for network security is the potential for false positives or negatives, network disruption or performance impact during scanning, and the inability to detect certain types of attacks such as insider threats. These limitations can be addressed by using a variety of security measures in addition to network scanning, such as access controls, intrusion detection and prevention systems, and regular security training for employees.

Quiz (Solutions in Appendix)

1. What were the main vulnerabilities and weaknesses exploited in the Target breach, and how could network scanning tools have been used to detect and prevent the attack?
2. How did the WannaCry ransomware attack use network scanning tools to propagate across networks, and what lessons can be learned from this attack for network security?

3. What were the main targets of the SolarWinds supply chain attack, and how did network scanning tools contribute to the success of the attack?

4. What are some best practices for using network scanning tools to identify potential vulnerabilities and security risks in a network?

5. How can network administrators use network scanning tools to improve network performance and management?

6. How can ethical hackers use network scanning tools to identify potential vulnerabilities and security risks in a network?

7. What are some potential risks associated with using network scanning tools, and how can they be mitigated?

8. How can network administrators use network scanning tools to ensure compliance with industry regulations and standards?

9. What are some potential limitations of network scanning tools, and how can they be addressed?

10. What are some potential limitations or drawbacks of relying solely on network scanning for network security, and how can they be addressed?

If you've read my book

If you've read my book, I would be grateful if you could take a moment to leave an honest review on Amazon. Your review will not only help other readers make an informed decision but also provide valuable feedback to me as an author. Thank you for taking the time to share your thoughts!

Introduction to Network Scanning Quiz Solutions

What are some of the ethical considerations when conducting network scanning activities?

Answer: Ethical considerations when conducting network scanning activities include obtaining permission to conduct the scan, ensuring that the scan is conducted within the limits of the law, and avoiding causing any unnecessary harm or disruption to the network.

What are some of the limitations of ping scanning?

Answer: Ping scanning has limitations in that it cannot identify open ports or services running on devices, and some devices may not respond to ping requests.

Why is port scanning an important part of the network scanning process?

Answer: Port scanning is important as it helps identify the open ports on devices that can potentially be exploited by attackers. By identifying open ports and the services running on them, IT administrators and security professionals can take steps to secure their networks and prevent potential attacks.

What are some of the common techniques used for service scanning?

Answer: Common techniques used for service scanning include banner grabbing, protocol scanning, and operating system fingerprinting.

What are some of the potential risks associated with network scanning activities?

Answer: Potential risks associated with network scanning activities include the potential for network congestion or impact on system performance, the possibility of triggering intrusion detection systems (IDS) or firewalls, and the potential for legal consequences if conducted without permission.

What is malware scanning and why is it important?

Answer: Malware scanning is the process of identifying malware and other malicious code that may be present on a network or device. It is important as it can help detect and remove malware infections before they cause damage to network resources or sensitive data.

What are some of the popular tools used for vulnerability scanning?

Answer: Popular tools used for vulnerability scanning include Burp Suite, Acunetix, and OWASP ZAP.

Why is operating system fingerprinting important in the network scanning process?

Answer: Operating system fingerprinting is important as it helps identify the specific operating system running on target devices, which can provide valuable information about potential vulnerabilities and security issues associated with specific operating systems.

What are some of the key considerations in the analysis and reporting phase of network scanning?

Answer: Key considerations in the analysis and reporting phase of network scanning include prioritizing vulnerabilities, determining remediation steps, generating a clear and concise report, and presenting the report to relevant stakeholders.

What are some of the benefits of network scanning for IT administrators and security professionals?

Answer: Benefits of network scanning for IT administrators and security professionals include identifying potential vulnerabilities, detecting malware infections, evaluating network performance, and taking steps to secure networks and prevent potential attacks.

Scanning Tools Quiz Solutions

What are the most popular scanning tools used for vulnerability assessment, and how do they differ from each other?

Answer: Popular scanning tools for vulnerability assessment include Burp Suite, Nessus, OpenVAS, and Nmap. Each tool has unique features and capabilities that differentiate it from the others.

How can ethical hackers use scanning tools to identify potential security risks and vulnerabilities in a network?

Answer: Ethical hackers can use scanning tools like Nmap or Burp Suite to identify open ports and services running on a network, and then use vulnerability scanning tools like Nessus or OpenVAS to identify potential vulnerabilities.

What are some of the ethical considerations that should be taken into account when conducting network scanning activities?

Answer: Ethical considerations when conducting network scanning activities include obtaining permission to conduct the scan, avoiding causing unnecessary harm or disruption to the network, and ensuring that the scan is conducted within the limits of the law.

How can operating system fingerprinting be used to identify potential vulnerabilities in a network?

Answer: Operating system fingerprinting can help identify the specific operating system running on target devices, which can provide valuable information about potential vulnerabilities and security issues associated with specific operating systems.

What are some of the potential risks associated with conducting network scanning activities, and how can they be mitigated?

Answer: Potential risks associated with network scanning activities include the potential for network congestion or impact on system performance, triggering intrusion detection systems (IDS) or firewalls, and potential legal consequences if conducted without permission. These risks can be mitigated by obtaining permission, conducting scans during off-peak hours, and using scanning tools that allow for customization of scan parameters.

How can scanning tools be used to identify malware infections on a network?

Answer: Malware scanning tools like Malwarebytes or McAfee can be used to identify malware infections on a network, and then take steps to remove the malware and prevent further infections.

What are some of the benefits of network scanning for IT administrators and security professionals?

Answer: Benefits of network scanning for IT administrators

and security professionals include identifying potential vulnerabilities, detecting malware infections, evaluating network performance, and taking steps to secure networks and prevent potential attacks.

How can network scanning tools be used to identify potential entry points for attackers to exploit?

Answer: Network scanning tools like Nmap or Masscan can be used to identify open ports and services running on a network, which can provide potential entry points for attackers to exploit.

What are some of the considerations that should be taken into account when selecting scanning tools for network security testing?

Answer: Considerations when selecting scanning tools for network security testing include the specific vulnerabilities and attack vectors being targeted, the level of customization and control needed, and the cost and availability of the tool.

How can ethical hackers use network scanning tools to collaborate with development teams to improve the security of web applications?

Answer: Ethical hackers can use web application scanning tools like Burp Suite or Nikto to identify potential vulnerabilities in web applications, and then work with development teams to implement secure coding practices and mitigate the vulnerabilities.

Host Discovery Quiz Solutions

What are some common techniques used for host discovery, and how do they differ from each other?

Answer: Common techniques used for host discovery include ping scanning, ARP scanning, and DNS enumeration. Ping scanning involves sending ICMP echo requests to network hosts, while ARP scanning involves sending ARP requests to discover hosts on a local network. DNS enumeration involves querying a DNS server to identify hosts on a network.

What are some of the benefits of conducting host discovery as part of a network security assessment?

Answer: Benefits of conducting host discovery as part of a network security assessment include identifying potentially vulnerable hosts, detecting unauthorized devices on the network, and improving network performance by identifying and resolving network congestion issues.

How can ethical hackers use host discovery tools to identify unauthorized devices on a network?

Answer: Ethical hackers can use host discovery tools like Nmap or Fing to identify devices on a network, and then compare the results to a list of authorized devices to identify any unauthorized devices.

What are some of the potential risks associated with conducting host discovery activities, and how can they be mitigated?

Answer: Potential risks associated with host discovery activities include causing network congestion or impact on system performance, triggering intrusion detection systems (IDS) or firewalls, and potential legal consequences if conducted without permission. These risks can be mitigated by obtaining permission, conducting scans during off-peak hours, and using scanning tools that allow for customization of scan parameters.

How can host discovery tools be used to identify potential vulnerabilities in a network?

Answer: Host discovery tools can be used to identify potential vulnerabilities by identifying network devices and analyzing the open ports and services running on those devices.

In scenario 1, what host discovery technique would be most effective for identifying potential vulnerabilities in the company's network, and why?

Answer: In scenario 1, a combination of ping scanning and ARP scanning would be most effective for identifying potential vulnerabilities in the company's network. This would allow the ethical hacker to identify all devices on the network, including those that may not respond to ICMP requests.

What are some of the best practices for conducting effective host discovery activities as part of a network security assessment?

Answer: Best practices for conducting effective host discovery activities include obtaining permission, using a variety of scanning techniques, scanning during off-peak hours, and analyzing the results to identify potential vulnerabilities.

In scenario 2, what host discovery technique would be most effective for identifying unauthorized devices on the network, and why?

Answer: In scenario 2, DNS enumeration would be most effective for identifying unauthorized devices on the network. This technique would allow the ethical hacker to identify all devices registered with the company's DNS server, and then compare the results to a list of authorized devices to identify any unauthorized devices.

How can host discovery tools be used to improve network performance?

Answer: Host discovery tools can be used to improve network performance by identifying and resolving network congestion issues caused by unauthorized or misconfigured devices on the network.

What are some of the potential limitations of host discovery techniques, and how can they be addressed?

Answer: Potential limitations of host discovery techniques

include devices that may not respond to ping requests or ARP requests, and devices that are hidden behind firewalls or other security measures. These limitations can be addressed by using a variety of scanning techniques, such as DNS enumeration or port scanning, and analyzing the results to identify potential vulnerabilities.

Port and Service Discovery Quiz Solutions

What are the benefits of conducting port and service discovery as part of a network security assessment?

Answer: Conducting port and service discovery helps identify potential vulnerabilities and security risks associated with specific ports and services running on network devices. It can also help network administrators identify unauthorized or misconfigured services running on the network.

What are some common techniques used for port and service discovery, and how do they differ from each other?

Answer: Common techniques used for port and service discovery include TCP and UDP scanning, banner grabbing, and port knocking. TCP and UDP scanning involve sending packets to target ports to determine if they are open or closed, while banner grabbing involves collecting information about a service running on a particular port. Port knocking involves sending a sequence of packets to a closed port to open it.

How can ethical hackers use port and service discovery tools to identify potential vulnerabilities in a network?

Answer: Ethical hackers can use port and service discovery tools like Nmap or Nessus to identify open ports and services on a network. They can then analyze the results to identify potential vulnerabilities associated with specific ports and services.

What are some potential risks associated with conducting port and service discovery activities, and how can they be mitigated?

Answer: Potential risks associated with port and service discovery activities include network congestion or impact on system performance, triggering intrusion detection systems (IDS) or firewalls, and potential legal consequences if conducted without permission. These risks can be mitigated by obtaining permission, conducting scans during off-peak hours, and using scanning tools that allow for customization of scan parameters.

How can port and service discovery tools be used to improve network performance?

Answer: Port and service discovery tools can be used to improve network performance by identifying and resolving network congestion issues caused by unauthorized or misconfigured services running on the network. This can help improve network efficiency and reduce the risk of downtime or performance issues.

In what scenarios would banner grabbing be the most effective technique for port and service discovery, and why?

Answer: Banner grabbing is most effective in scenarios where the attacker has limited access to the network or is attempting to remain undetected. This is because banner grabbing provides information about a service running on a specific port without sending large amounts of traffic to the network.

How can port knocking be used to prevent unauthorized access to a network?

Answer: Port knocking can be used to prevent unauthorized access to a network by requiring a specific sequence of packets to be sent to a closed port before it can be opened. This can make it more difficult for attackers to gain access to the network.

What are some best practices for conducting effective port and service discovery activities as part of a network security assessment?

Answer: Best practices for conducting effective port and service discovery activities include obtaining permission, using a variety of scanning techniques, scanning during off-peak hours, and analyzing the results to identify potential vulnerabilities.

How can network administrators use port and service discovery tools to identify misconfigured or unauthorized services running on the network?

Answer: Network administrators can use port and service discovery tools like Nmap or Nessus to identify open ports and services on the network. They can then compare the results to a list of authorized services to identify any unauthorized or misconfigured services running on the network.

What are some of the potential limitations of port and service discovery techniques, and how can they be addressed?

Answer: Potential limitations of port and service discovery techniques include the use of non-standard ports, firewalls or other security measures that may block access to certain ports or services, and false positives or negatives. These limitations can be addressed by using a variety of scanning techniques, such as banner grabbing or port knocking, and analyzing the results to identify potential vulnerabilities.

Scanning Beyond IDS and Firewall Quiz Solutions

What are some of the limitations of intrusion detection systems (IDS) and firewalls in detecting and preventing network attacks?

Answer: IDS and firewalls can be limited in detecting sophisticated attacks that use evasion techniques or disguise themselves as legitimate traffic. They may also fail to detect attacks that are executed within the perimeter of the network.

What are some common techniques used for bypassing IDS and firewalls?

Answer: Common techniques for bypassing IDS and firewalls include packet fragmentation, protocol manipulation, traffic encryption, and tunneling.

How can ethical hackers use port scanning tools to identify open ports and services on a network?

Answer: Ethical hackers can use tools such as Nmap or Nessus to perform port scans on a network to identify open ports and services running on network devices.

What are the benefits and limitations of using vulnerability scanners as part of a network security assessment?

Answer: The benefits of using vulnerability scanners include the ability to quickly identify potential vulnerabilities on a network. Limitations include the potential for false positives and the need for periodic updates to the vulnerability databases.

What are some best practices for conducting effective vulnerability scans as part of a network security assessment?

Answer: Best practices for conducting effective vulnerability scans include obtaining permission, using up-to-date scanning tools, conducting scans during off-peak hours, and analyzing the results to identify potential vulnerabilities.

How can ethical hackers use social engineering techniques to bypass network security measures?

Answer: Ethical hackers can use social engineering techniques, such as phishing or pretexting, to trick users into divulging sensitive information or granting access to restricted areas of the network.

How can network administrators use intrusion prevention systems (IPS) to detect and prevent network attacks?

Answer: IPS can be configured to detect and block network attacks in real-time by using predefined signatures and heuristics to identify suspicious network activity.

What are some of the potential risks associated with using honeypots and decoys as part of a network security strategy?

Answer: Potential risks associated with using honeypots and decoys include diverting valuable resources away from critical network assets and providing a false sense of security if not properly managed.

What are some common techniques used for obfuscating network traffic to bypass IDS and firewalls?

Answer: Common techniques for obfuscating network traffic include encryption, tunneling, steganography, and traffic shaping.

How can network administrators use a layered approach to network security to protect against sophisticated attacks that bypass traditional security measures?

Answer: A layered approach to network security involves using multiple security measures, such as firewalls, IDS, IPS, vulnerability scanners, and access controls, to detect and prevent network attacks.

Draw Network Diagrams Quiz Solutions

What is the purpose of creating a network diagram, and how does it help in a network security assessment?

Answer: The purpose of creating a network diagram is to provide a visual representation of the network infrastructure, which helps in identifying potential vulnerabilities, mapping network traffic flows, and improving network management.

What are some common tools and techniques used for drawing network diagrams, and how do they differ from each other?

Answer: Common tools and techniques used for drawing network diagrams include pen and paper, Microsoft Visio, Lucidchart, and network mapping software. The tools differ in terms of their features, ease of use, and pricing.

What are some best practices for creating effective network diagrams as part of a network security assessment?

Answer: Best practices for creating effective network diagrams include using standardized symbols and labels, updating the diagrams regularly, including all relevant network components, and keeping the diagrams organized and easily accessible.

How can network diagrams be used to identify potential security risks and vulnerabilities in a network?

Answer: Network diagrams can be used to identify potential security risks and vulnerabilities in a network by mapping network traffic flows, identifying single points of failure, and identifying network components that are not properly secured.

What are some common challenges that may arise when creating network diagrams, and how can they be addressed?

Answer: Common challenges when creating network diagrams include incomplete or outdated information, difficulty in identifying all network components, and the need to update the diagrams regularly. These challenges can be addressed by using automated network mapping tools, working closely with network administrators, and conducting regular reviews of the diagrams.

How can network diagrams be used to improve network performance and management?

Answer: Network diagrams can be used to improve network performance and management by providing a clear overview of the network infrastructure, identifying bottlenecks and other performance issues, and facilitating efficient network management.

What are some potential risks associated with creating and sharing network diagrams, and how can they be mitigated?

Answer: Potential risks associated with creating and sharing network diagrams include the risk of unauthorized access to sensitive network information and the risk of inadvertently exposing vulnerabilities. These risks can be mitigated by restricting access to the diagrams, encrypting sensitive information, and properly disposing of outdated diagrams.

How can network diagrams be used to ensure compliance with industry regulations and standards?

Answer: Network diagrams can be used to ensure compliance with industry regulations and standards by providing a clear overview of the network infrastructure, identifying areas that are not compliant with the standards, and facilitating the implementation of required security measures.

How can network diagrams be used to support incident response and disaster recovery efforts?

Answer: Network diagrams can be used to support incident response and disaster recovery efforts by providing a clear overview of the network infrastructure, identifying critical network components and dependencies, and facilitating efficient restoration of services in the event of a network outage.

How can network diagrams be used to improve communication and collaboration between different stakeholders in a network security assessment?

Answer: Network diagrams can be used to improve communication and collaboration between different stakeholders in a network security assessment by providing a clear and standard-ized representation of the network infrastructure, facilitating discussion and agreement on network security measures, and improving overall understanding of the network environment.

Network Scanning in Action Quiz Solutions

What were the main vulnerabilities and weaknesses exploited in the Target breach, and how could network scanning tools have been used to detect and prevent the attack?

Answer: The Target breach exploited vulnerabilities in the company's payment systems and network segmentation, which allowed the attackers to move laterally across the network and steal sensitive data. Network scanning tools could have been used to identify weaknesses in the network segmentation and to detect any suspicious network activity that may have indicated a potential attack.

How did the WannaCry ransomware attack use network scanning tools to propagate across networks, and what lessons can be learned from this attack for network security?

Answer: The WannaCry ransomware attack used network scanning tools to identify vulnerable systems running outdated software and then exploited these vulnerabilities to propagate across networks. The attack highlights the importance of keeping software up to date and using network scanning tools to detect vulnerabilities and potential security risks.

What were the main targets of the SolarWinds supply chain attack, and how did network scanning tools contribute to the success of the attack?

Answer: The main targets of the SolarWinds supply chain attack were government agencies and companies that used SolarWinds' network management software. Network scanning tools were used to identify vulnerable systems and to deliver the malware through software updates, which contributed to the success of the attack.

What are some best practices for using network scanning tools to identify potential vulnerabilities and security risks in a network?

Answer: Best practices for using network scanning tools include conducting regular scans to identify potential vulnerabilities, using up-to-date scanning tools, analyzing scan results to prioritize vulnerabilities, and implementing security measures to address identified risks.

How can network administrators use network scanning tools to improve network performance and management?

Answer: Network scanning tools can be used to identify bottlenecks and other performance issues in the network, as well as to track network activity and monitor network performance over time. This information can be used to optimize network configurations and improve overall network management.

How can ethical hackers use network scanning tools to identify potential vulnerabilities and security risks in a network?

Answer: Ethical hackers can use network scanning tools to identify open ports, weak passwords, outdated software, and other potential vulnerabilities and security risks in a network. This information can be used to recommend and implement security measures to prevent malicious attacks.

What are some potential risks associated with using network scanning tools, and how can they be mitigated?

Answer: Potential risks associated with using network scanning tools include triggering intrusion detection systems or firewalls, causing network congestion or impact on system performance, and potentially exposing sensitive information if not properly secured. These risks can be mitigated by using customized scan parameters, scanning during off-peak hours, and implementing proper access controls and encryption measures.

How can network administrators use network scanning tools to ensure compliance with industry regulations and standards?

Answer: Network scanning tools can be used to identify areas of the network that are not compliant with industry regulations and standards, such as weak passwords or outdated software. This information can be used to implement required security measures and ensure compliance with regulations and standards.

What are some potential limitations of network scanning tools, and how can they be addressed?

Answer: Potential limitations of network scanning tools include false positives, incomplete or outdated information, and the need for periodic updates to scanning databases. These limitations can be addressed by using a variety of scanning techniques, verifying scan results with additional testing, and keeping scanning tools and databases up to date.

What are some potential limitations or drawbacks of relying solely on network scanning for network security, and how can they be addressed?

Answer: Some potential limitations or drawbacks of relying solely on network scanning for network security include the potential for false positives or false negatives, the possibility of network disruption or performance impact during scanning, and the inability to detect certain types of attacks such as insider threats. These limitations can be addressed by using a variety of security measures in addition to network scanning, such as access controls, intrusion detection and prevention systems, and regular security training for employees. It is important to use network scanning as part of a comprehensive network security strategy rather than relying on it as the sole measure.

OS Discovery Quiz Solutions

What is OS discovery and why is it important in a network security assessment?

Answer: OS discovery is the process of identifying the specific operating system running on network devices, which is important in a network security assessment to identify potential vulnerabilities and security risks associated with specific operating systems.

What are some common techniques used for OS discovery, and how do they differ from each other?

Answer: Common techniques used for OS discovery include banner grabbing, operating system fingerprinting, and protocol analysis. Banner grabbing involves analyzing the banner message sent by network services to identify the operating system running on the device. Operating system fingerprinting involves analyzing network packets and responses to identify the specific operating system running on the device. Protocol analysis involves analyzing network protocols to identify the specific operating system running on the device.

What are the benefits and limitations of using banner grabbing for OS discovery?

Answer: The benefits of using banner grabbing for OS discovery include simplicity and speed, while limitations include the potential for false positives and the reliance on the accuracy of the banner message sent by the network service.

What are the benefits and limitations of using operating system fingerprinting for OS discovery?

Answer: The benefits of using operating system fingerprinting for OS discovery include greater accuracy and the ability to detect operating system versions, while limitations include the potential for false negatives and the need for more sophisticated tools.

How can ethical hackers use OS discovery tools to identify potential vulnerabilities in a network?

Answer: Ethical hackers can use OS discovery tools like Nmap or Amap to identify the specific operating system running on target devices, which can provide valuable information about potential vulnerabilities and security issues associated with specific operating systems.

What are some potential risks associated with conducting OS discovery activities, and how can they be mitigated?

Answer: Potential risks associated with OS discovery activities include causing network congestion or impact on system performance, triggering intrusion detection systems (IDS) or firewalls, and potential legal consequences if conducted without permission. These risks can be mitigated by obtaining permission, conducting scans during off-peak hours, and using scanning tools that allow for customization of scan parameters.

How can network administrators use OS discovery tools to improve network security and performance?

Answer: Network administrators can use OS discovery tools to improve network security and performance by identifying potential vulnerabilities associated with specific operating systems and implementing security measures to address them. They can also use OS discovery tools to identify misconfigured or outdated systems that may be impacting network performance.

What are some best practices for conducting effective OS discovery activities as part of a network security assessment?

Answer: Best practices for conducting effective OS discovery activities include obtaining permission, using a variety of scanning techniques, scanning during off-peak hours, and analyzing the results to identify potential vulnerabilities.

How can the use of honeypots and decoys improve the effectiveness of OS discovery activities?

Answer: The use of honeypots and decoys can improve the effectiveness of OS discovery activities by diverting attackers away from critical network resources and providing false information about the network to discourage further attacks.

What are some potential limitations of OS discovery techniques, and how can they be addressed?

Answer: Potential limitations of OS discovery techniques include the use of obfuscation techniques to hide the true operating system, the presence of virtualized or containerized environments that may appear as different operating systems, and the need for advanced tools to accurately identify the operating system. These limitations can be addressed by using a variety of scanning techniques and analyzing the results to identify potential vulnerabilities.

www.ingramcontent.com/pod-product-compliance
Lightning Source LLC
LaVergne TN
LVHW022124060326
832903LV00063B/3794